Abundance of Love

Archdiocese
of Oklahoma City
Library

MINDENTIM

Abundance of Love

The Incarnation and Byzantine Tradition

by

Archbishop Joseph Raya

Educational Services
Diocese of Newton
West Newton, MA 02165

Originally published, 1989, in conjunction with the annual convention of the Melkite Greek Catholic Eparchy of Newton.

Second printing, 1990.

(c) 1989, Archbishop Joseph Raya
All Rights Reserved

Library of Congress Cataloging-in-Publication Data

Raya, Joseph, 1917-

Abundance of love: the Incarnation and Byzantine tradition / by Joseph Raya
p.   cm.
Includes bibliographical references.
ISBN 1-56125-015-5
1. Catholic Church - Byzantine rite, Melchite - Doctrines.
2. Incarnation. 3. Word of God (Theology) 4. Catholic Church - Byzantine rite, Melchite - Liturgy. I. Title.
BX4711.334.R393 1989
281'.5 --dc20   89-77803

Table of Contents

Foreword iii

Introduction 1

Part One: The First Incarnation 7

1. Perfect God and Perfect Man 9
2. The Story of the Incarnation 21
3. The Radiance of the Incarnation 31
4. The Temple of God 51

Part Two: The Second Incarnation 73

5. The Holy and Divine Gospel 75
6. Proclamation of the Gospel Message 86
7. The Gospel in the Liturgy 95
8. The Royal Road: Asceticism 107
9. Moral Asceticism 116
10. The Kingdom 131

Illustrations

The Theotokos, Byzantine Museum, Athens*	7
The Annunciation**	23
Detail of Christ, Agia Sophia, Constantinople	32
St. Joseph's Church, Akron, Ohio	55
Holy Transfiguration Church, McLean, Virginia	58
St. John the Baptist Church, Northlake, Illinois	63
Christ Enthroned, Byzantine Museum, Athens*	73
Reading of the Gospel, St. Joseph's, Akron	88
St. Luke the Evangelist	106

*(Courtesy of * God With Us Publications, ** Rev. Kenneth Sherman; others courtesy of Sophia Press.)*

The Cover

These Royal Doors from the Byzantine Museum, Athens illustrate the various "incarnations" of the Logos in Christian experience. The annunciation icon (upper center panels) represents His incarnation in the flesh. The icons of the prophets which flank it recall the incarnation of the Word in the Scriptures. The icons of the liturgical Fathers below indicate His incarnation in the worshipping Church. *(courtesy of God With Us Publications).*

Foreword

"Preserving our Tradition" - What can this mean for us as Eastern Christians in the modern, Western world? Is it the retention and propagation of the language or habits of our ancestors? Is it the imitation of the externals of another culture so as to protect our faith in a hostile environment? Certainly other Christian groups, both Eastern and Western, have suggested that this is so.

In the prologue to his book *The Orthodox Way*, Bishop Kallistos (Timothy Ware) suggests another course. "... loyalty to Tradition means not primarily the acceptance of formulae or customs from past generations, but rather the ever-new, personal and direct experience of the Holy Spirit *in the present*, here and now." We are true to authentic Tradition, then, when we experience in a living and active way the reality of God's presence to which the elements of Tradition are signposts.

It is in this spirit, I believe, that the present book was written. Its author, Archbishop Joseph Raya, has had ample opportunity to experience the presence of God in a variety of circumstances. Serving as Archbishop of Nazareth and all Galilee, he lived in the midst of the smoldering tension between Israeli and Palestinian which has captured the headlines in the past year. Currently serving the troubled eparchy of Marjayoun in southern Lebanon, he seeks to communicate this vision to a people driven to and fro as refugees through their beleaguered country during a decade of Christian-Muslim conflict.

Despite these oppressive circumstances, Archbishop Joseph has remained a person of joy and faith: a spirit which he seeks to share with us in these pages so that the Gospel basis of our vibrant Tradition may enliven our own lives as it has his own.

All who read this work are indebted as well to Father August J. Deasio and Saint Joseph's parish of Akron, Ohio, hosts of the 1989 Diocesan Covention, for making publication of this book possible.

Rev. Fred Saato
Director of Educational Services
Eparchy of Newton

Introduction

At this point of our history it is imperative to communicate with each other, to be in personal relation, to uncover and discover the most intimate secrets of our lives. Imperative also to share our religious experiences in the infinite love that God has for his creation. All of us human beings yearn to share both the fever of our insecurities and the glory of our personalities. Presidents, political giants, as well as artists and actors, share their "confessions" in a new literary form called "memoirs."

Our Lord shared his "memoirs" also. The holy and divine Gospel Book is the gift of himself to the world.

In this present book I share with you, dear reader, what the Eastern Byzantine Church has discovered and experienced of the life and love of the Lord. I am giving you in this book an account of the fruits of her prayer, contemplation, the echo of her silence before God. It is also my own experience and the fruit of my prayer and contemplation.

Theologians, artists and poets, together with saints and monks of two thousand years, combined their geniuses to produce a theology, an iconography, and a hymnology, unmatched in the literary history of mankind. Byzantine theology, liturgy, and the icon are not the product of one nation or one culture. They express East and West, far East and far West, Africa and the arid Eskimo lands. All the nations and cultures find in them today an echo of their mind and heart because icon, liturgy, and hymnography are expressions of the sublime and the beautiful.

The intrinsic qualities of the sublime are the unmeasured, the dynamic, and the serene. The sublime appeals to the intellect, to the imagination and to all the appeals to the intellect, to the imagination and to all the human faculties; it directs them towards the inner mystical and spiritual world. The sublime belongs to an even higher level of being than the beautiful. It is a pure spiritual beauty. All cultures and levels of civilization are attracted by the sublime which characterizes Byzantine religious expression.

There is a great mystery in human experience. There is a greater mystery yet in religious experiences. At one time we thought that patient analysis and scientific formulations could express and release such religious experiences. Theologians forgot the feast, the sublime and religious experience. They wrote books on how to pray and how to worship, just as others wrote books on how to construct a machine, or organize a corporation. Can a book really teach how to pray or how to swim? Is not praying like swimming, a "letting go"? Swimming is really an act of confidence that cannot be taught or commanded. The water itself, while carrying us, rewards the confidence we have put in it. One day, on the first swim or on the hundredth, we notice that we do not sink: we move along in the water.

So it is with praying. In the course of listening to the voice of the Beloved we feel, one day, that we really are inhabited by a flame. Reason will stop her activity and give way to a much superior one, to an activity with a special intensity of presence and communication. In prayer we enter into the mystery of life where God reveals himself to us and where we find our human dignity and infinite divine value. In such a relation of life with God we become superior human beings who can "let go" and thus attain to the summit of "knowledge," to the feast, to religious experience. This book is the unfolding of religious experience, of the feast of Christ and of the superabundance of love of our God.

Byzantine ceremonial and liturgies are the water that will carry anyone into religious experience and into the joy of the feast. Byzantine ceremonies are poems that every one can read and delight in, though not necessarily understand.

Introduction

They are the "letting go." They are poetical inspirations that can communicate life and invite to the sharing of life.

I was not yet born when my blood started praying. Our Melkite mothers believe that the water of their womb bubbles with the flame of the Holy Spirit. The day my mother knew she was entrusted with a new life, she started singing and praying every day the office of my Byzantine Church. She sang those melodies all during the nine months of that happy expectation. The process of my religious experience started in the womb.

Every day my mother borrowed the liturgical books of the season from the parish church, and every day she returned them to our octogenarian priest for his own use. Melodies succeeded melodies as feasts came and went. Every day in the womb I was lulled by sighs of praise, adoration, and penance.

Christmas had just passed when I inhabited the womb. Then came Epiphany, followed by the Meeting of the Eternal with Simeon and Anna; next the Incarnation and the Great Holy Week. For my expectant mother, the time of the Resurrection that year must have been more glorious than glory because my whole being, my flesh and my sinews, for the past seventy years of my life (and I hope that this will continue until my last breath), have thrilled with a special tingling whenever I hear or sing "Christ is risen!"

The feast of the Ascension followed in its turn, and then the Descent of the Spirit, then Transfiguration. A winter, a spring, and half a summer had come and gone in lightning rapidity.

On August the fifteenth, the day of the Assumption or the Falling Asleep of the Theotokos, at the break of dawn, while the bells of the thirty-three churches in my village were peeling their carillons, filling the valley with sounds of joy, I came into this world with the cry of all newly born: "Here I am!"

My mother, like all Melkite mothers when they have a baby, held me up high in her arms to the Icon of the

Blessed Mother of God, while the midwife shouted the good news to all those who were waiting outside the room of my birth. The cantor of the Church, who had been hired for the occasion, intoned the Troparion of the feast of the Assumption of the Mother of God, which was repeated several times by everyone present:

In Your maternity
You did retain your virginity!
And even though you ascended to heaven,
You did not forsake the world.
O Mother of God, you were transferred to life
Because you are the Mother of Life.
Through your intercessions
save our souls from death.

Since that happy moment of my life, every time I utter a prayer to the Mother of God, the Troparion of her Assumption rings clearly and loudly from every pore of my being. Blessed be that moment when my humanity was plunged into the best "Catechism" the Christianity of East and West has ever invented, the Troparion.

In my early childhood I learned how to play the game of God and of the Church, and how to swing the censer and make its bells ring in unison. Our priests in town were all Basilian monks, Salvatorians. They were holy, peaceful, and faithful heralds of good news. Our Salvatorian priests never allowed children to "play church" at home. The real church was always open for our holy games. There we played as deacons, priests, and even bishops! Those who could read, used the books. The others mumbled and babbled. Every child sang joyously, heartily, and sometimes, as children are wont to do, rowdily! We never had an official "catechism." But we could recognize the saints in their Icons. We could light a candle, walk in procession, and sing troparia with clapping hands and stamping feet. It was my first "Letting go," the bright dawn of a long day of years of my religious experience.

Trust and confidence reigned supreme in our relations with our priests. A priest for us Melkites is not a name only, a "Father." He is a face, he belongs to us. He is "our father," "my father," "Abouna." The favorite saying of our octogenarian Abouna Clement was: "My children, study every line and every color of the Icons. Icons are beauty and goodness! I want you to be beautiful and good!"

His other saying that stuck to my flesh was: "Remember children, that the Christian does not go to heaven! The Christian does not possess heaven! It is heaven that dwells in the Christian and possesses the Christian! Heaven is in you, in your inner being, not out there somewhere!"

Later in my youth I went to the seminary of the White Fathers in Jerusalem. Like all seminarians who were in modern seminaries, I learned how to conquer heaven! Seminarians were given innumerable books of theology and philosophy, and were constantly taught how to prove doctrines and convince others by syllogisms and intellectual demonstrations. Religious experience was called "sentimentality." We had to despise and shun personal feelings and experiences. We belittled our liturgical books in favor of Aristotle and the Summa of Saint Thomas.

But we were beset with difficulties along every step of this religious process of learning. I remember that I was engulfed by doubts like many of my fellow seminarians. I suffered intolerable anxieties because I knew that the logical, historical, theological, philosophical, and psychological "proofs" of the textbooks did not really prove anything. The few who could master intellectual syllogisms and abstractions were proud of their intellectual powers. Sometimes they became haughty, and quite often bored with religion. Those who could not excel intellectually became confused and sometimes resentful. The seminary was a sad place. Intuition and self-expression were carefully monitored or suppressed.

After the Second Vatican Council, the Tridentine seminary program has been somewhat revised and "modernized." But it is still a sad place to prepare for the priesthood of Christ. The little joy and freedom that belonged to our "ancient" seminary has succumbed to the "university" model. "Credits" and "accreditation" have killed the feast and whatever was left in our soul of light-heartedness. The seminary is still a very sad place!

We will be redeemed only when we will learn how to celebrate and how to proclaim the feast of Christ.

+Archbishop Joseph Raya

Part One - The First Incarnation

The Son of God
Becomes Son of Man

1. - Perfect God and Perfect Man

In the fullness of time, the Son of God becomes Son of Man. At a point in history when humanity was ready to receive the radiant splendor of God's glory, the Poet-Creator and Lover came down from heaven, assuming human form in the womb of a young girl of our race. "When the fullness of time had come," says St. Paul, "God sent forth his Son, born under the law" (Gal. 4.4).

GOD BECOMING MAN

The Son of God, the God of God and Light of Light, took on our physical reality. He became a fetus growing and developing as does every human being. The Creator became matter: the Infinite was contained in a womb. "The Word was made flesh," says St. John (1, 14). God the Son joined us in our humanity while keeping his own distinct divine nature and unity in the Trinity.

We call the feast of March 25 by a double name. If we stress the event of God becoming man, we call it Incarnation. And if we stress the event of the Archangel Gabriel proposing to Mary that she become the Mother of God and obtaining her consent, we call it Annunciation.

In 453 the Fourth Ecumenical Council of Chalcedon defined with majesty the reality of the Incarnation. The Fathers of the Council gave us a declaration which is in fact a hymn to God, stressing the dignity of the human person:

We teach that the one and only Son of God,
our Lord Jesus Christ,

> *is the very same one perfect in divinity,*
> *and very same one perfect in humanity.*
> *He is the very same God,*
> *consubstantial with the Father*
> *according to his divinity,*
> *and the very same person,*
> *consubstantial with us according to his humanity.*
> *He is the one and same Christ in two natures*
> *(human and divine).*
> *without change, without confusion,*
> *without division, without separation.*
> *The union of the two natures*
> *did not in any way suppress*
> *the difference between these natures:*
> *each one kept its proper character and distinction*
> *while encountering the other in the unique Person,*
> *in the one and unique Lord, Jesus Christ,*
> *the unique Son of God, himself God the Word.*

The Council Fathers make two major points. First, the union of God with our human flesh is a real, physical union, whereby the nature of God is united to our human nature; secondly, that this union of the divine and the human is most special, such that one nature is not overwhelmed or changed by the other. The Divine remains Divine, and the human remains human, yet the union is most complete. Christ is both perfectly human and perfectly God. Through this special union humanity becomes by grace what God is by nature.

The first point is affirmed by St. Paul: "In Christ the fullness of deity resides in bodily form" (Col. 2,9). There is no change in Christ's divine nature, no becoming, no turning from one kind of nature into another. When assuming human nature, the Person of the Word of God, the Logos, the second Person of the Trinity, remained God as he always was and will remain forever, but at the same time he was really in the flesh. God became a participant in our human experiences. We can truly say that God was incarnate in the flesh, that God was born, thirsted and hungered, that God suffered, and died and is risen, and that God ascended into heaven. St. Gregory Nazianzen sings of the true Man and the true God, both present in Christ's Incarnation:

> *He was born,*
> > *but he was already begotten;*
> *he came forth from a woman,*
> > *and he kept her a virgin.*
> *He was wrapped in swaddling bands,*
> > *but he removed the swaddling clothes of the*
> > *grave when he rose from the dead.*
> *He was laid in a manger,*
> > *but he was glorified by angels,*
> > *and proclaimed by a star,*
> > *and worshiped by the wise Magi.*
> *He had no form of beauty in the eyes of his people,*
> > *but to David, he was fairer than all the children*
> > *of men.*
> *On the Mountain, he was bright as the lightning.*
> > *He became more luminous than the sun,*
> > *illuminating us into the mysteries of the future.*
> *He was baptized as a man;*
> > *yet he remitted sins as God.*
> *He was tempted as a man,*
> > *but he conquered as God.*
> *He suffered hunger,*
> > *but he fed thousands.*
> *He knew what it was like to thirst,*
> > *but he cried: 'If any man thirst,*
> > *let him come to me and drink.'*
> *He experienced weariness,*
> > *but he is the peace of all who are sorrowful*
> > *and heavy-laden.*
> *He prays,*
> > *yet he also hears prayer.*

He weeps,
> *but puts an end to tears.*
He asks where the lifeless Lazarus is laid,
> *for he is a man;*
And he raises Lazarus from the dead,
> *for he is God.*
As a sheep he is led to be slaughtered,
> *but he is the Shepherd of Israel,*
> *and also of the entire world.*
He is bruised and wounded,
> *but he heals every disease and every infirmity.*
He is lifted up and nailed to the tree,
> *but by the tree of life he restores us.*
He lays down his life,
> *but he has the power to take it up again.*
He dies,
> *but he gives life, and by his death*
> *effectively destroys death.*
> > *(Oration 29)*

St. Paul calls the way God appeared in our flesh *kenosis*. Kenosis means that God "emptied himself" from all the glorious emblems of his divinity. He did not abandon his divinity, but covered up its glory, and became subject, not only to the general limitations of human nature, but also to the historical circumstances of a definite period and race. The Eternal submitted to time, and the Law-giver to the law of Moses: "He was born of a woman, made under the law" (Gal. 4,4). God remained God as he always was, and our humanity was penetrated by divinity. We can consequently say that, for Christ, who is the Man-God, or rather God-Made-Man, nothing human could ever be alien.

MAN BECOMING GOD - DIVINIZATION

Because of the real union of the Person of God with our nature, every power and passion of the human body is, in its essence, a noble, holy, and sacred melody. God the Father gave a human nature to his Son. The human body is, therefore, the most precious gift God can offer - besides his own Self. "We saw his glory" in the naked body of a Baby. For Christians, human flesh is a present and a reward, a divine instrument by which God saved and divinized the whole universe. When he ascended into heaven in that very same flesh, he carried us and the universe to the Father, our source and origin. This is our divinization.

This most important teaching of our Christian religion has been forgotten or neglected "because of our preoccupation solely with our own salvation: or, rather, union with God is seen only negatively, in contrast with our present wretchedness" (V. Lossky, *In the Image and Likeness of God*, pg. 99).

In uniting with our nature God did not change himself, and he did not obliterate humanity either. He offered himself as a grace and a gift to our humanity and elevated it to a higher level of being. He divinized us, which means that he gave us the grace and capacity to love and to live his own love and life.

It is by this favor of divinization that we can think and love and act like God. It is a pure gift, the gift of a sacred life with him. No creature by itself could ever think, or love, or act on the level that is proper to God. But by coming to us and joining himself to us, God has enabled us to think and to love as he does, to be truly like him, to be one in mind and heart with him. Athanasius of Alexandria said it so well: "God came to bear our flesh in order that we may become bearers of the Spirit."

In the Incarnation our humanity was robed with a divine character and a divine splendor, and the matter of the universe became a "divine milieu" where God lives and breathes life and love. When we freely and directly offer our own personality to Christ and accept his way of life, perfect union is accomplished with him, and divinization becomes operative in all its effects. This doctrine of divinization is the primary idea of the declaration of the Council of Chalcedon.

UNITY OF THE DIVINE AND THE HUMAN

The second idea stressed at the Council of Chalcedon is that this union of the divine and the human is not an amalgamation or absorption, where one thing neutralizes or obliterates the other. The Divinity remained entirely intact in the humanity, and humanity remained completely effective when united with divinity. Divinity was hidden and embedded in humanity. This is kenosis; and humanity was thus divinized.

The sanctification or divinization of humanity consists, therefore, primarily and above all, in the gift of God's indwelling in us. God himself has chosen to become the center of our every thought, decision, and desire. He has given us himself in the most intimate closeness of union. He dwells in us, as in his own temple, and abides in us, as in his own milieu. He becomes our own holiness. The value of our religious acts comes not from what we do, but from our faith, love, and hope, from our awareness of God as seeing, caring, and communicating himself to us, so that we can live his life and communicate it to others.

FLESH, SIGN OF UNITY

As a consequence of this sublime teaching, the Council of Chalcedon proclaims that the humanity of Christ is not only the humanity of an individual, Jesus Christ, but the humanity of everyone. According to the Bible and Christian understanding, the expression "God became flesh" means that God became matter. He became really human, with a real human body and soul and everything that pertains both to the process and the structure of being human; it also includes all the surprises of human existence.

"Flesh" also means the physical part of the universe, the same stuff of which the stars and planets and the interstellar dust particles are made. Hence "flesh" points to and signifies union with the whole created universe as well as unity and solidarity with every human being.

The word "flesh" has an inner relationship, if not an essential identity, with another concept of both Old and New Testaments: "dust." The words flesh and dust designate, in both Testaments, the whole man. They designate the whole man precisely in his basic "otherness" to God, in his frailty, in his intellectual and moral weakness, in his separation from God, which is manifested in sin and death. The two assertions "man is flesh" and "man is dust" are, then, more or less essentially similar assertions.

The symbol of dust was used in the Bible as a declaration of man's essence: "From the earth you were taken; dust you are, and to dust you shall return" (Gen.2,19). Dust is the image of the whole man body and soul, even if it applies in different ways: "God is mindful that man is only dust" (Ps. 102,14).

The good news of salvation rings out: "The Word became flesh." He became dust. He became what we are. In Christ, "flesh" and "dust" designate not only a descending movement into nothingness, into sin and death, but an ascending movement as well, an elevation to eternity, to immortality and to God. The downward motion into flesh and dust has become for us an upward motion, an ascent to the highest heavens, a divinization.

When the Gospel says that the Logos, God, became "flesh," it means that every single human being "in the flesh" has been penetrated by divinity and united to God. When God became Man, man and all humanity became sharers of the divinity and partakers of Christ's divine attributes. There was an ineffable exchange between God and humanity; but in this exchange humanity remained what it is, a creature, and God remained who he is, Creator and God of all.

According to this sublime understanding, which was Christ's understanding, human flesh (*sarx*) is, therefore, a sign, a symbol, and the visible reality of the invisible unity of all mankind, and indeed of the whole material universe. As the flesh of Adam was sign and symbol of the unity of all creation, so the flesh of Christ, "the second Adam," is sign and symbol of the unity of all humanity and of the whole creation.

THE FIRST ADAM

The story of Adam and Eve shows us that as long as Adam was in perfect harmony and peace with God, harmony and peace remained everywhere. Paradise and perfect bliss reigned. The whole creation was at peace because of its unity with Adam. But when Adam lost that harmony and peace in himself, he also lost paradise. Paradise was lost for all of us and for all creation precisely because of the solidarity and unity of Adam with the rest of creation. The story of Adam's fall into sin, and of the consequences of his sin, exemplifies the biblical belief in the interdependence and solidarity of all flesh.

THE SECOND ADAM

Saint Paul says that Christ, the Son of God, is for humanity and for creation the Second Adam. Christ is the Second Adam because he sums up the whole of human history. In him mankind went back, as it were, to its beginning, in order to set out afresh on its journey to maturity, which will be reached when we all come together in him, to form a single perfect man (Eph. 4,3).

In him all things were made new, and a radical reorientation in humanity and in creation was set in motion. All people now become one body with Christ, and Christ becomes one person with humanity. St. Cyril, commenting on St. John's Gospel, says. "The only begotten Son of the Father has the whole of the Father in his nature. When he became flesh, he blended, as it were, with our human nature, through an ineffable union with our earthly body .... He is at the same time God and man. He unites in himself, in some way, what is most different by nature and makes it a sharer of the divine nature."

UNITY AND SOLIDARITY OF ALL FLESH

In his Epistles, St. Paul explains this unity and solidarity of all flesh and matter in the light of some practices God has ordered Moses to follow and to keep faithfully. God has ordained that the first fruits of every crop should be offered to him, and that the first-born male child of the family be also surrendered to him. St. Paul says that the offering of the first fruits to God signifies that all subsequent fruits and products also belong to God. The offering of the first-born of the family means the offering of all those who will be born from the same womb. The whole family belongs to God. The Jewish saying was: "One in all and all in one."

Explaining this doctrine further, St. Cyril of Jerusalem says: "Even different and separate as we were, the Only Begotten of the Father devised a means to fuse and unite us in his Incarnation as he unites us also in the reception of his Body. Who can divide those Christ has united to him? Who could deprive them of their physical union, when they are bound together in unity with Christ by means of his holy Body?"

Gregory of Nyssa insists that in the light of the Incarnation Christians should stress strongly and insistently the truth of the unity of all flesh in Christ. "Our unity is so real," says Gregory, "that one cannot talk about 'men' in the plural anymore, as we cannot talk about plurality in God when we say 'Father-Son-Spirit!'"

We Christians live in harmony with others because we are conscious of our union with Christ and with all others. We are able to love and to forgive because we know from experience that we are all one. We are in touch with others because we are conscious of our union with Christ. We are in touch also with the cosmos, and we affirm the goodness of everything and of every one, because we see the unity of everything in him. He is the reality of all that is real.

THE GREEK NOTION OF FLESH

The Greek philosophical notion of "sarx" and matter is contrary to this sublime biblical understanding. For Greek philosophy, matter and "flesh" are composed of parts. Parts limit and are limited. They have boundaries, and they make boundaries. Consequently, they are elements of division. Since the human body is composed of parts which limit and disintegrate, the Greek philosophers believed it is unworthy of the immortal soul that inhabits it. They saw the human person as an incarnate soul, not, as in the Bible, an animated body. Consequently, for them, body and soul were enemies.

According to Plato, the soul, which does not die or disintegrate, was in God before the creation of matter. When the soul fell into sin, God punished it by throwing it into the material body in which it became "incarnated" as if it were in a prison. For Plato, therefore, since the body is a prison, it has to be despised, punished, and even eliminated, to allow the soul to fly back to its origin. Gnosticism and manicheism developed this Greek philosophy into a system of behavior which became so powerful that it penetrated and infected Christian minds for centuries. "Flesh," which is a real glory for the Gospel and for Christianity, became synonymous with an enemy of God. Recurring in Western theology is the idea that three enemies of God are "the world, the flesh, and the devil."

CHRISTIAN NOTION OF FLESH

In the biblical and Christian understanding, human persons are not "incarnate souls; they are, instead, "animated bodies." Body and soul are wedded in love. The body is a bride. The body is penetrated with God's goodness. God joined body and spirit, not out of punishment, but out of love. For us Christians, the body is a part of the universe and represents the whole universe. It is a tent and a dwelling place of God's delight. It was out of love that God created the body, and it was out of love that he assumed the body. Thus, when he united our body and creation in himself, he restored them to their pristine glory, and returned them to the Father who is their Source.

The unity and solidarity of the whole creation is in the flesh of Jesus Christ. This truth is the golden thread that runs through our whole Christian teaching, giving it a meaning and relevance we can never repeat enough. When God the Son became incarnate, he joined in himself heaven and earth, and united the Creator to his creation. Consequently, when he died for our sins, humanity died in him and with him. Sin was wiped out and destroyed. When he rose from the dead, all humanity rose in him and with him and shared in his new life. And when Christ God "ascended into heaven and sat at the right hand of the Father", in him and with him our humanity was restored to its original beauty. Humanity and creation flowed from the love of God-Trinity; in Christ God they were returned to God-Trinity.

It makes sense, therefore, to say that the sacraments convey the grace or life of God because the sacraments are made of the matter of creation which is already united with God through the Incarnation, alive in him through the Resurrection, and filled with him through the Ascension. Since matter has thus been penetrated by divine reality, a piece of bread can become Eucharist and contain and impart the Living God; water can be a channel for God's life and for identification with Christ in baptism; a drop of oil in Chrismation can impart the Holy Spirit; and an Icon can be the Sacrament of Christ and bearer of the Spirit!

In the Incarnation, Christ became the essence of humanity, the center of creation, the focal Being in relation with all beings. The Incarnation is the pure act of love by which God desired to be one with his creation.

The Fathers of the Eastern Church constantly affirmed that God would have become man even if Adam had not sinned. God made the universe out of love, not out of necessity. He is rightly called *Philanthropos*, a Lover, the Lover of his creation and of every human face in this world. The reason for his Incarnation does not proceed from sinful mankind in need of salvation, but from God, who is a Lover, Abundance of life and love. He became flesh because of his desire to manifest his divinity in humanity, which he created to be the beloved place of his presence.

2. - The Story of the Incarnation

Let us now read the facts as they are related in the Gospel:

And in the sixth month the angel Gabriel was sent from God to a town of Galilee called Nazareth, to a virgin betrothed to a man named Joseph, of the house of David, and the virgin's name was Mary. And when the angel had come to her, he said, 'Rejoice, highly favored of God. The Lord is with you. Blessed are you among women.' When she had heard him she was troubled at his word, and kept pondering what manner of greeting this might be. And the angel said to her, 'Do not be afraid, Mary, for you have found grace with God. Behold, you shall conceive in your womb and shall bring forth a Son, and you shall call His name Jesus. He shall be great and shall be called the Son of the Most High; and the Lord God will give Him the throne of David, His father, and he shall be king over the house of Jacob forever; and of His kingdom there shall be no end.'

But Mary said to the angel, 'How shall this happen, since I do not know man?' And the angel answered and said to her, 'The Holy Spirit shall come upon you, and the power of the Most High shall overshadow you; and therefore the Holy One to be born shall be called the Son of God.' But Mary said, 'Behold the handmaid of the Lord; be it done to me according to your word.' And the angel left her." (Luke 1, 24-38). And the word of God became flesh and He dwelt among us (cf John 1, 14).

The Son and Word of God, God of God, became thus personally a man, and he personally assumed all the complexities involved in the historical individual life of a man. The Timeless One intersected with time, and the history of humanity became a history of God. Only silence and adoration can absorb the majesty of Incarnation.

THE ICON OF THE INCARNATION

The story of the Incarnation as related in the Gospel, is manifest in all its majesty of colors and awesome movements in the Icon of the Incarnation. This icon is a gentle scene, a silent beauty of attitudes, colors, and secret conversation. The historical fact that happened in Nazareth two thousand years ago is remembered, and becomes a present reality in the icon.

The Virgin Mary occupies the right side of the icon, the Archangel Gabriel, the messenger of God, the left. Heaven faces earth, and earth is wrapped up in the mystery of God, who is proposing to establish a new relation with his creation.

Mary and the archangel are placed against an architectural background which indicates that the event took place on earth. Mary is in a space suggesting a house, and the archangel Gabriel stands in front of a high tower representing heaven. At the top both places are united by a red silken shawl. Heaven is joined to earth, and earth becomes heaven. The Holy Scripture is wide open on a lectern. Mary has just finished reading the prophet Isaiah's cry of hope for the coming of the Messiah: "Drop down, ye heavens, from above, and let the skies pour down righteousness: let the earth open, and let them bring forth salvation . . . " (Isaiah 45,8).

In this icon we find ourselves at the moment when Mary has accepted the invitation of God and has pronounced her *fiat*: "Let it be done to me according to your word" (Luke, 1,33). Life cannot be imposed: it is offered. Nicolas Cabasilas explains:

The Story of the Incarnation

"*The Incarnation was not only the work of God, but also that of the will and faith of the Virgin. Without the consent of the Most Pure, without the collaboration of her faith, the plan of God would have been as impossible to realize as it would have been without the intervention of the three divine Persons themselves. God has chosen her for his mother and borrowed the flesh she willingly accepted to surrender to him. As he was incarnate of his own free will, he wanted his mother to give him birth as freely and willingly.*" (Homily on the Annunciation)

New Eve, Mother of God, Mother of all living. It is for all of us that Mary pronounced her fiat.

The archangel is bowing to her in awesome reverence and gratitude for her acceptance, and from a corner of heaven the Holy Spirit descends to overshadow her and fill her with grace.

By the window just above Mary's head red flowers raise their petals in a proud, upward sweep, expressing the delicate texture of the female figure standing in glory before God who is asking a favor; and yet her attitude is an attitude of humility.

In Byzantine churches this icon of the Annunciation is generally placed on the Royal Doors of the iconostasis, the gate way to the Holy of Holies. This beautifully represents the reality that it is only through Christ the Way, who took flesh at this awesome moment, that we have access to the inaccessible God. To complete the dogmatic meaning of the Incarnation, the four Evangelists are often represented on the Royal Doors as well. They are seated at their lecterns, writing their Gospels. This signifies that as the Holy Spirit descended upon Mary to effect the Incarnation of the Son of God as Son of Man, so also he descended upon the Evangelists to effect the Incarnation of the Word of God as the word of man - a Book, the Gospels.

THE LITURGY OF THE INCARNATION

What the Gospel reveals, the icon paints in colors and beauty, and the liturgy sings in glory. The liturgy stresses all the divine aspects of the mystery, and proclaims them in marvelous literary forms:

> *Today is the announcement of joy,*
> *Today is the virginal festivity,*
> *Today heaven is joined to earth,*
> *Adam is renewed in life,*
> *And Eve released from sorrow.*

The dwelling place is our own substance
Which has become God's temple
And which has been thus deified!...
(Doxastikon at the Vigil)

The Feast of the Annunciation is one of the most important feasts of the Christian year. The Church has been celebrating this feast since the third century. St. Athanasius (353) in his sermon on this feast calls it "the first in the list of feasts." Emperor Mauricius (582) made it obligatory in the whole empire, and the Church of Rome adopted it somewhere between the years 660 and 680.

The liturgy celebrates the divine drama in all its details. Heaven opens a window to earth, and Nazareth becomes the place of the mystery that even angels cannot understand. How can God unite with his creation, and how can a girl of our human race conceive without man's participation?

These are questions our minds can't answer as they cannot answer the miracle of the first creation. How did God make all creation from nothing? But in God all these miracles are like a melody that he has been humming from all eternity. He made the first Adam out of the earth. And now he makes the second Adam out of the flesh of a woman. The first woman came out of a rib of Adam. The second Adam, who is God of God, came out of the entire being of a woman.

To say that the Holy Spirit "overshadowed her" means that he permeated every fiber of her body and drew from her most intimate reality a new human nature, more perfect and more glorious than the humanity of the first creation. Adam was male-female. Mary was female-divine-male. It was only when God invented tenderness that he divided Adam so that woman could appear in her own proper female reality which is tenderness, harmony, and meaningfulness. It was only when God decided to reveal his infinite love for human beings that he took on our human flesh and became a human reality to make humanity divine. Adam was put to sleep to give birth to woman. Mary was awakened to accept God in her flesh. She had to hear the offer of God. She had to respond to his invitation.

HEAVEN FACES EARTH

The miracle of the Incarnation is described and sung in its many splendored efficacy in the liturgy. The office is a continuous song of exultation that awakens emotions and desires that belong to the transcendent order of being. It is replete with affirmations which reveal the mysterious character of the union of God with his creation. Let us listen to the conversation between Mary and the angel and see how the divine was at work:

"The Archangel Gabriel was sent down from heaven to announce to the Virgin that she would conceive. He came down over Nazareth, meditating in his heart, bewildered by this wondrous event, and saying: 'How can the One beyond understanding, the Most High Himself, come to be born of a Virgin? How can the One whose throne is heaven, and to whom the earth serves as a footstool, ever be contained in a woman's womb? How could He have condescended to be incarnate of her at a single word that only she can say? He upon whom the Six-winged and Many-eyed Seraphim are not allowed to gaze?"

And the archangel solves for all humanity the hesitations of our intelligence and the problems of our human logic:

"He who is coming is the Word of God! Why do I hesitate? I shall say to the Maiden: 'Rejoice, O woman full of grace! The Lord is with you. Rejoice, pure Virgin! Rejoice, O Bride and Maiden ever-pure! Rejoice, O Mother of Life! Blessed is the fruit of your womb!" (Doxastikon at Vespers)

The Virgin must answer the invitation of God in the name of all humanity. She is fearful, she asks questions, she hesitates because she is human and does not want to surrender blindly to a seemingly impossible adventure. Mary hesitates and warns the Archangel not to mislead or deceive her.

"The virginal Maiden replied to the Captain of the heavenly hosts: 'You come to me in human form; Why then do you speak in words beyond human understanding, saying: "The Lord is with you," and "The Lord will dwell in your womb." Explain to me how I am to become a spacious vessel, for the One who is above the Cherubim. Mislead me not, for I know no pleasure of the flesh, nor do I know man: How then shall I give birth to a Son?' (Sticheron at vespers)

The conversation of Mary with the archangel illuminates the divine action and gives it significance unsuspected before. The archangel has no explanation. All he can offer is the act of faith that the event is God's work and God's will:

The Bodiless One answered the Maiden and said: 'Whenever God so desires, He can overcome the laws of nature: what is impossible to man may be accomplished by Him. Wherefore, O woman most Holy and pure, believe the truth of my word...'

EARTH FACES HEAVEN

Mary heard the words of God "and pondered them all in her heart" (Luke 2, 52). The word of God is for her a treasure and a seed that grows immediately into life. She accepts his offer because God is the One who offers and who is offered:

"...She answered and said: 'Be it done to me according to your word, and I will give birth to the Bodiless One who will

take flesh from me, so that by His union with a body, man may be raised to the original state of grace, for he is almighty."'
(Sticheron at vespers)

Mary's strong personality and grandeur of character are all in this dialogue. In her there is nothing primitive, no sweet-scented banality or weak pietism. She is not a little girl, docile, blindly obedient, and all submissive to a domineering male as she was stereotyped by the piety of the Middle Ages. Her femininity towers above the archangel and borders on the divinity. She also stands tall and strong against all human odds. She realizes all the dangers of her situation of pregnancy without a legal husband. But once she was assured that it was God who was the Lover, she accepted his action in her and courageously turned her face towards society, the synogogue, and the man to whom she was promised. Without boasting or arrogance, humbly and chastely, she opened her womb to God and hurried to her cousin Elizabeth to share the good news with her.

THE HYMN OF GLORY

Elizabeth recognized in Mary the chosen one and the "blessed among all women." She even humbled herself before the youthful mother of her Lord: "How is it that I deserve to be visited by the mother of my Lord!" (Luke 1,43). With great dignity Mary gave to the One who had chosen her and expressed in fiery words the grandeur of her feminine dignity which no woman ever thought herself able to possess. She said:

My whole being magnifies the Lord.
My heart rejoices in God my Savior.
He has overcome my limitations.
Behold all generations shall call me blessed.
The Mighty Himself has done in me great things,
Holy He is, and his faithfulness is forever.

The Story of the Incarnation

> *He has done marvelous deeds,*
> *He has done marvelous deeds,*
> *and scattered the proud in their conceit.*
> *He has put down the mighty from their thrones*
> *and has exalted the humble.*
> *He has filled the hungry with good things,*
> *and the rich He has sent empty away.*
> *He has received Israel, his servant,*
> *because his love is forever faithful,*
> *As He had said it to our Fathers:*
> *to Abraham and to all his generations forever.*

The Byzantine Church does not sing this hymn without interrupting every verse to magnify her who sings of the glorious deeds of her God. After every verse we interject this expression of our admiration and praise:

> *Higher in honor than the Cherubim,*
> *and more glorious beyond compare than the Seraphim:*
> *In virginity you gave birth to God the Word.*
> *You are truly the Mother of God:*
> *You do we exalt.*

God does not deal in ideas. He does not reveal abstract concepts. God reveals himself. He gives himself. In the Old Testament, he reveals himself to Moses as Master and Law-giver; in the prophets, as Lover, Savior, and Protector of his people. In the New Testament, God reveals himself in human flesh and in a human face. He reveals himself in Jesus Christ who is a Son of our human race. The self-revelation of God is always explosive. The human answer to the call of God is wonder, followed by thanksgiving and self-surrender. It is expressed by hymnography, and the icon paints it in colors and sacred silence.

In my younger days I regularly visited holy monks. One day I came to the Monastery of St. Elias of Windows in Zahle. Hieromonk Clement had the Icon and the Gospel opened to the event of the Annunciation of the Incarnation. A week later I found him in contemplation before the same icon of Mary and the angel. Another week later he was still on the same page of the Gospel, in front of the same icon. I dared to ask: "Father, you have been reading the same page and looking at the same icon for more than two weeks!" "Son," he said, "when I come to these words, 'Be it done to me according to your word,' I see God becoming man. The whole world lights up for me. I see that all human beings are my brothers and sisters. I see them radiate holiness and goodness. In the icon all the elements of creation are penetrated and sanctified by the Incarnation of God. I contemplate his divine glory, and I come to know that his Incarnation is salvation and redemption for the whole world. I become myself a flame of holiness and do not feel the need to contemplate anything else."

3. - The Radiance of the Incarnation: The Icon and Its Meaning

The icon is the beautiful and necessary extension of the Incarnation. The word "icon" means "image," or "reflection," the mirror where we experience a person and the image where we recognize the face of God in our human appearance. Saint Paul says that "Christ is the Icon of the invisible God" (Col. 1, 15). He is the Icon of the Father because he shows us the Father. "He who has seen me has seen the Father" (John 14, 9), the Lord said to Philip. Christ is indeed the Revelation of God the Father.

The underlying idea of the Icon is the manifestation of the hidden. "I represent God, the invisible," says the Damascene, "not as invisible, but insofar as he has become visible for us by participating in our flesh and blood. I do not represent the invisible deity but I represent the flesh of God which has been seen." (*The Orthodox Faith*)

In depicting the Savior, we do not depict either his divine nature or his human nature, but his Person, in which both natures are united in an incomprehensible way. The icon is the representation of the person, not of the nature. "Essence, (or nature) has no independent existence," says John of Damascus, "but is seen in persons" (*The Orthodox Faith*, Book 3, Ch. 6). Icons give us the possibility of communicating with the Person of the Son of God, and of knowing the Person of the Son of God, in the historic fact of his Incarnation. Icons are the gift of the Incarnation.

LIGHTING IN THE ICON

The light that shines in the icon by which we see faces and events is unlike the light of day by which we see people and objects in ordinary life. In the icon we see by a divine light, the light that springs from the risen Lord who is himself "the Light of the world." When we look at icons we can never tell where light comes from. Does it come from this corner or that corner? From above or from below?

From sun or moon or stars? In the icon light has no visible source. Its only source is Christ radiating through every face, through every garment, and through every object represented. The Holy Spirit resides in every detail of the icon, and it is the Holy Spirit also who permeates all, and shines forth and radiates from every thing. The Holy Spirit is the totally luminous source of light. He shines through the flesh and the folds of clothes, and he bathes everything with loveliness.

Bodies are represented as having been restored to their pristine beauty and harmony. They are the expression of the victory of Christ over death and dissolution, and his triumph over division and chaos.

Our Christian religion is not simply a doctrine or an intellectual pronouncement. It is not a formula, but an action and a fact. "The very fact of the existence of the icon," says L. Ouspensky, "is based on the divine fact of the Incarnation. And the immutability of the fact of the divine Incarnation is affirmed and demonstrated by the icon ..." (*The Meaning of Icons*, p. 34). God the Lord is made manifest in the peace and harmony of colors and secret movements, and man is shown transfigured and divinized, illuminated in all the details of his body. The icon is, therefore, the transfiguration of creation as shown in the face of Jesus Christ who is very Divinity, one with the Father and the Spirit.

The cosmos also is soaked through and through with a special divine presence and conveys God's goodness. The cosmos is the pearl and the divine milieu of God. It participates in the divinity and grace, exempt from sensual quality or corruption. Matter has no heaviness in the icon. It is soaked with grace and reaches to the heavens.

The seventh Ecumenical Council of 787, the Second of Nicea, teaches that the "icon was not the invention of artists, but the faithful reproduction of the special Spirit that lives in the heart of the Christian and in the tradition of the Church." The icon is a witness to the Incarnation and to the reality of the divinization of the whole creation. It is existentially identical with its model, while being essentially different. Every color, movement and representation is a silent proclamation of what the Gospel says in words. The icon does not teach: it reveals the Divine Life and the hidden meaning of human words and human events.

THE ICON AND THE INCARNATION

A concise exposition of the meaning of the icon is sung in the kontakion of the Sunday of Orthodoxy, the first Sunday of Great Lent. The kontakion is addressed to the Mother of God to explain her own presence in the Icon:

> *The uncircumscribed Word of God became circumscribed.*
> *When He was incarnate in You, O Mother of God,*
> *He restored our corrupt image to its former beauty*
> *by joining it to his divine splendor.*
> *Wherefore we now proclaim our salvation,*
> *and make it known by word and deed.*

The first part of this kontakion discloses the connection between the icon and the Incarnation, although the two are essentially different. In his divinity the Son of God is uncircumscribed because he is the consubstantial image of the Father. But in his humanity he is circumscribed and reveals that he is an authentic human being. The reality of the One Person in him ensures the unity of the two natures "without change, without confusion, without division, without separation" (Fourth Ecumenical Council of Chalcedon). In the icon we do not have humanity separated from divinity. Christ is one Person, the Person of the Son of God, the Second Person of the Trinity. As God he is uncircumscribed. But when he became incarnate he became circumscribed in our flesh. He became a human being - matter - to divinize matter and humanity by giving them the power and the possibility to be vehicles of holiness.

The second part of the kontakion affirms that because we have been thus divinized and "restored to our former beauty," we are capable of saving matter and making it an instrument of salvation. We participate in the divine character of Christ, and we receive the power to reveal him in words (like in the Gospels), and in deeds (like in the icon).

The icon is the visible Gospel, the silent proclamation of whoever Christ is, of whatever he represents. The Council of 860 states that "all that is uttered in words (in the Gospel) ... is also proclaimed in the language of colors (in the icon)" St. John of Damascus further explains that "just as in the Bible we listen to the words of Christ and thus we are sanctified ... so it is with the painted icons: we behold the representations of his human form, of his miracles and passion, and are likewise sanctified, and fully reassured, and imbued with joy, and pronounced blessed ...." By joining our nature to his divine splendor, Christ made us capable of creating an external icon of him with the matter that surrounds us; capable of creating an icon of him in words - the Gospel.

Besides being a witness to the Incarnation, the icon is also a proof and a pledge of the Christians power to redeem creation. St. Paul writes that "the whole nature groans in common travail to be set free from the tyranny of corruption, to share in the glorious freedom of God's sons" (Rom. 8, 21).

THE ELEMENTS THAT MAKE UP THE ICON

In the icon all the elements of the material creation converge to unite with the breath of man for sanctification and redemption:

- The plant is present in the wood panel;

- The mineral world is in the chalk and alabaster that cover the wood; it is also in the paint, in the jewels, and in the other precious materials used;

- The animal world is also present in the egg yolk which the iconographer mixes on his palette of twenty-four basic colors;

- Finally, the human element consists of the relics of saints which the iconographer adds, whenever it is possible, to the paint.

Thus the whole visible world enters into expressing the invisible and the divine.

Once all these elements are put together, the artist's hands purify them with the breath of the Spirit Who is in him. The matter is revivified and saved and brought forward to serve its Creator. It becomes a liturgical object and a channel of grace. Every icon is called "miraculous" because it is "soaked with divine energy and grace, which is the presence of the Holy Spirit, and it leads to the grace of sanctification" (John of Damascus, *Treatise "On the Icon"*, 1, 16). Within the Church the icon becomes a way for spiritual and bodily therapy, just as the Bible is the Word of God, "quick, and powerful, and sharper than any two-edged sword" (Heb. 4, 12).

The Second Council of Nicea decreed that icons are to be venerated in the same manner as the Holy Scriptures since icons, and Scriptures alike are reflections of the same Revelation. They both express the inexpressible God, who became expressible in the Incarnation. Icons participate in the fullness of his presence in the flesh. As the Holy Scriptures reproduce his Revelation in words, icons reproduce him in colors and in the harmony of human forms. The Fathers of this Council clarified the doctrine further by saying, "What we have heard in the Holy Scriptures, now we see in the icons." What the word proclaims, the icon exposes in the silence of the human face. St. Ignatius of Antioch had long before declared that "he who possesses in truth the word of Jesus can hear even its silence!"

Considered in itself, the icon has no particular significance; it is wood and matter. But considered in the light of the Incarnation, and sharing in the breath of the Holy Spirit, it reveals the hidden, and shares in the reality of Christ's redemption. The Seventh Ecumenical Council declares explicitly again that "by contemplation of Scripture and by the icon . . . we are introduced into the presence of the prototypes and we are in their very presence".

At this Council the Fathers established a clear distinction between the icon in itself, which does not receive any consideration, and the veneration of what it represents, which is the face and figure of the God who made matter and became incarnate in it. Saints and angels in the icon are only the radiance of his face. In contemplating the icon we identify with this radiance and we receive grace from it through the process described by St. Paul saying, "We who have no veil over our face contemplate as in a mirror the splendor of the Lord, and we are transformed into his image" (2 Cor. 3, 18).

St. John of Damascus, the greatest theologian of the icon, says: "He who denies that God can be present in matter must also deny the Incarnation of Jesus Christ." And he specified further, saying, "I worship the Creator of matter, who, for my sake, became material and dwelt in matter, and through matter effected my salvation. I will not cease worshiping him through the matter in which my salvation has been effected."

HISTORY AND DEVELOPMENT OF THE DOCTRINE OF THE ICON

Since the days of Constantine the Great, faithful Christians have rendered honor to icons, statues, and images representing Christ, his holy Mother, and the saints and martyrs. Such practices, however, encountered heavy opposition, particularly on the part of the Jews and Muslims. The Jews regarded them as a grave infraction against the law of Moses (Exodus 20, 4), and the Muslims referred to the Koran, which forbids any representation of God, or of any living creature.

In some way these restrictions are right and just because in pagan religions idols are pictures of things which do not exist. Since they are not real in themselves the matter that represents them becomes the sole object of worship. This is idolatry. But in the icon Christ reveals God in his very divine Person, real and present in our human face. He is the true image of God the Father (2 Cor. 4, 4; Col. 1, 15; John 14, 9). In the face of Christ we see and encounter the Father.

Furthermore, what added strength and purpose to the opposition to icons was the misguided conception and superstitious practices some Christians displayed towards icons. They treated them as real idols, believing that they were, by themselves, intercessors, invested with divine powers and capable of miracles without connection with the prototype. Naturally, many holy monks and learned bishops, as well as zealous fellow Christians, were led by this distorted behavior to believe that such a veneration of the icons was a return to paganism. They opposed their use and their legitimacy.

Under the influence and pressures of these circumstances Emperor Leo III the Isaurian (717-740), decreed in the year 726 that the cult of images was forbidden in the Empire. He ordered the icons to be destroyed, thus deserving the name "iconoclast," or destroyer of icons. His son, Constantine V (740-775), gave rise to bitter and violent controversy. He called a Council in 754 which decreed: "We declare unanimously in the name of the Holy Trinity, that there should be rejected and removed and cursed out of the Christian Church every likeness which is made out of any material whatever by the evil art of the painters."

The Radiance of the Incarnation

Sacred ornaments were trampled under foot, liturgical vessels turned to profane use, and churches scraped down and smeared with ashes because they contained holy images. Monasteries were confiscated, and monks arrested, imprisoned, or exiled. Some died in prison. Others were exhibited in grotesque exhibitions in the hippodrome where they were paraded alongside harlots and forced to marry.

After the death of Leo IV in 780 there was a brief respite for the Church. Empress Irene, his wife, became regent. She was an "iconophile," a supporter of icons. During her husband's life-time she could do little, but on her accession to the throne she issued an edict for liberty and freedom of conscience, and gradually she replaced iconoclast bishops with monks who had retained their love for icons.

The empire was too strongly iconoclast to be won over quickly, and the eastern boundaries of the empire, all three Melkite patriarchates, were still under Muslim attack, or dominated by iconoclast armies.

In 787, the Seventh and last Ecumenical Council restored the veneration of images, and Leontius explained the Orthodox position to the meeting in these words:

> "I, worshiping the images of God, do not worship the material wood and colors, God forbid; but laying hold of the lifeless representation of Christ, I seem myself to lay hold of and to worship Christ through it . . . for the honor of the image passes on to the original and he who worships the image worships in it the person of Him who is therein depicted."

In spite of the gigantic efforts Irene displayed in re-establishing devotion to icons, her victory was a fragile one. In 815 Leo V reaffirmed the tenets of the anti-icon Council of 754. Persecution and intolerance troubled the Church again until the conflict ended in 842 under Empress Theodora. The icon triumphed. The joy of Christians was so intense that they started hanging icons in profusion on the screens of the sanctuaries (icon-screens), on the walls of churches, and in their homes.

In the year 843 the synod of Constantinople instituted for the first Sunday of Lent a special celebration to commemorate the triumph and the meaning of the holy icon, and in the year 1166, at the Synod of Blachernae, this celebration of the icon was extended to include the celebration of the triumph of the "true faith" over all past heresies, and the Sunday was called the "Sunday of Orthodoxy."

CANDLE LIGHT

Because they represent and manifest divine realities, icons are hung on walls, placed on altars and on special stands, or set permanently in elaborate shrines. In the presence of the icon burns a lamp or a candle, a symbol of life. The candle or lamp light reminds us that the Lord is light - "I am the Light of the world" (Math. 5, 14).

The living flame before the icon symbolizes also the emotions of thanksgiving, self-revelation, tenderness, generosity, illumination and warmth. Lit candles and lamps in front of icons also symbolize the waiting for the moment of the encounter with the beloved Lord. The flame flickers and dances to the music of the face of the One who made himself visible, and who became the Lover of every human face. The flame captures our attention and bids us wait for the moment of the encounter with him: "See that you are dressed for action and your lamp lit . . . Happy those servants whom the Master finds awake when he comes" (Luke 12, 35).

THE ICONOGRAPHER

Because the icon is intrinsically holy, and a sign and symbol of holiness, it demands that the artist responsible for its creation should be holy and devout. For this reason icons

The Radiance of the Incarnation

are generally painted by monks, or by families who, for generations, have dedicated themselves to this holy art.

Iconographers must be steeped in theology as well as in liturgy, for the icon is both theology and liturgy revealed in images. "For we speak of it from contemplation," says St. Simeon the new Theologian, "therefore, that which we relate should be called a record of what has been contemplated rather than an idea" (*Discourse 63*, Par. 3, as quoted by Ouspensky, op. cit. p. 14). In Byzantine times the icon painters called their word "the prayer of contemplation."

An icon does not transmit ideas, or things to meditate upon, but Truth itself, the divine truth of God. "How is it possible," says the New Theologian again, "that anyone could speak or proclaim anything about God if he were not first illumined by the light of God." Only those who have experienced God can reveal God. The creation of an icon is, therefore, the fruit of asceticism, prayer, and contemplation, the work of the holy and wholly dedicated artist.

Tamara T. Rice says that iconographers "are concerned to convey the religious fervor which serves as the mainstream of their life, striving to demonstrate their faith with such a radiance that its incandescent might succeed in kindling a like devotion in those who gaze upon their paintings" (*Russian Icons*, p. 15). The rule is that they must spend forty days in prayer and contemplation before setting their artistic abilities into motion. Only after having thus prepared themselves and all the materials for their work do they submit these materials to the Church, who then solemnly blesses them and launches them on their way to realization. Real iconographers do not sign their work. They are supposed to have been liberated from self and from the lust for praise. They know that they are only instruments of the Holy Spirit who inhabits them and who alone manifests the meaning of Christ and the events of his life.

The icon is stripped of everything that is personal to a specific painter. The artist cannot say, "This is the way I see it . . . " but, "This is the way it is!"

If the name of the artist-painter cannot be put on the icon, the name of the person or the event represented in the icon must always be inscribed to identify it. Without a name the icon is incomplete and invalid. It is the written name of the person or persons, or of the subject represented, that transforms the icon into a valid picture for worship. Patriarch Nicephorus says that the "name written on the image sanctifies the icon."

THE BODY IN ICONOGRAPHY

A true icon must reveal both humanity and divinity. It cannot, therefore, be a mere photographic representation or a copy of what the naked eye alone can perceive.

The icon represents the transfigured and glorified body which is the visible expression of the Resurrection. St. Paul says that the transfigured body is not like the earthly body: it is "spiritual," glorified and penetrated by the light of the Resurrection. All the senses of the person represented in the icon have been refined, illumined, and bathed in the light of God. The colors of the paint are bright, blazing with the splendor of the rainbow. The background is of gold, for gold is the symbol of heaven and reminds us that those who are represented in the icon abide in heaven where God resides and where spiritual bodies are at home.

Body and flesh are two distinct things. The icon paints a body without even suggesting the flesh, or "carnal house." It represents the risen body and the final triumph of the flesh in simplicity and clarity.

The body is without even a hint of roundness, having neither volume nor weight, and supported by nothing. It is not even a part of the landscape. It is free and independent from the physical surrounding. It floats in spiritual space where prayer and adoration have completely abolished distances.

The Radiance of the Incarnation

In order to reproduce in the personages the heavenly atmosphere where they now reside, iconographers avoid practices and expressions that might show turbulent feelings. They seek calm and clarity in all the human emotions. Henceforth the icon is full of peace and majesty. The gestures and movements are serene. They do not gesticulate or display any haphazard action. No heavy sensuality or disturbing emotions can enter in.

Because heavenly, and living in the Holy Spirit and by the power of his breath, the personages are not in profile. They look straight into our eyes. Sometimes they are represented on an angle, three quarters only. This is to give the impression that they are in motion, advancing towards us or towards a central figure. Their feet extend sometime beyond the frame of the painting so they appear to come out and join us where they can visit and be visited. This same dynamism is expressed in their robes and veils which sometimes float or trail behind as if wafted by the air. The feet are hardly touching the ground. Feet and hands are elongated and small to denote sensitivity.

THE FACE

The faces are the most important part of the icons. The faces have the burning eyes of mystics and the long noses of ascetics. The lines of the mouths are beautifully silent, charged with profound secrets which only the eyes can reveal. The features of the faces are elongated, stretching out towards the heavens. The eyes are large, directed straight into our eyes with an attentive look. They try to penetrate to the depths of our consciousness, to awaken us or to inspire us. If they look towards heaven it is to contemplate a vision of glory. They look taller than they would on earth. They are lifted up to a higher level of being.

The countenance in the icon never expresses any distorted feelings such as anger, sickness, suffering, or any extravagant moods of sadness, or even of joy, or any other sentimental mood like that of an aimless reverie. The countenance is always calm, bathed in the Holy Spirit, and sustained in peace by his presence. The crucified attitude of the Lord, for example, is always full of majesty and grandeur even in the most painful moment of his death.

If the faces and all the attitudes of the icon show gravity and seriousness, they have nothing of indifference, of absence, which characterize the Far Eastern art of India and of paganism in general. The faces of icons are in relationship with us. They speak to us. They reveal to us. They display for us and offer for our own contemplation a lyrical quality, a gentleness, and an openness full of dignity and grace. They show us harmony and peace.

The halos around the head are symbols and representations of an intense life that fills the person and bursts out from his whole being into glory. The halos are the radiance of the intensity of life that is in them. For this reason, the halos are always in gold, or in silver, signifying divinity.

There are two types of halos, a round one, most common in all icons; and the kind suitable only to Christ, which consists of two geometrical figures divided into four corners symbolizing Christ who is Life, Light, The Way, and Final Salvation.

RESEMBLANCE

Because the icon is a sacramental liturgy, theology demands that the persons or events it represents remain true to the original. The image must be a resemblance because it expresses a specific original, and points to a special object. Because it is a representation it must have a resemblance with the original. The resemblance identifies the prototype. Holy canons insist that artists be faithful to this resemblance. Thanks to this the human eye will be able to rise to celestial spheres and capture in spiritual contemplation the original. Thus we are introduced to sacred realities and the icon will channel the grace of the original. The style be-

The Radiance of the Incarnation

longs to the artist, and it can vary from one generation to the next, and from culture to culture, but the face that belongs to the person represented must resemble the original.

Even the colors are subjected to laws which are inspired partly by the liturgy and partly by tradition. They cannot be chosen at random. Almost all icons go back to an archetype which has remained the norm from the very beginning. According to tradition, these prototypes originated through divine inspiration, or in some special miraculous way. The Apostle Luke, to whom special icons of Mary are attributed, is supposed to have been the first who inaugurated these artistic canons.

THE BACKGROUND

The icon is an awesome work of art, an expression of theology, whose spiritual power is within. It represents an inner transfiguration and leads to inner transfiguration.

In the icon, personages and events are considered to be in heaven. They live and move in the *kairos* of God, ever flowing, ever present, in "spiritual space." They are in heaven and lead us to heaven. It is from the Holy Spirit and in the Holy Spirit that they acquire infinite extension and duration, and it is the Holy Spirit who endows them with the grace to be present and to be real. Because the Holy Spirit cannot be confined or limited in a physical space, they also are free from physical confinement and limitation.

We know that the events of the life of Christ happened two thousand years ago in a spacial, historical condition. In his life on earth Christ was born in a grotto. He lived in a house. He entered the temple. He was surrounded by mountains on land, and by water in a river or a lake. Christ, the Son of God and God of God, was, in his human reality, confined in physical localities and circumscribed in every movement of his life. But now he is risen and glorified, yet as real and as alive as ever before. All his actions of two thousand years ago are still "anointed" and penetrated by the

Holy Spirit. He and his actions are no longer limited by geographical space or specific areas.

In the icon, historical scenes of two thousand years ago are indicated in the background only, while the personages and their actions are in the open space, free from any geographical limitation. They *are* and they are *actual* in the Holy Spirit.

The contemplation of the icon fills the mind and the heart with the mystery of Christ and awakens us to the presence of the Holy Spirit. This saying of our forefathers in the faith was a primary law of psychology: "You become what you contemplate." In the icon we indeed contemplate the beauty of the face of God in redeemed matter. We are bound to become what we contemplate. In the contemplation of the icon beauty and harmony are treasures that cannot be buried. They become our own treasures.

In summary we can say that the icon is the mirror of the Incarnation, a concrete example of matter redeemed and restored to its original beauty and harmony, one of the first fruits of resurrection and transfiguration.

St. John of Damascus calls the icon:

> a revelation and a song of triumph,
> a channel of grace!
> a life that emanates power,
> and inspires hope!
> and gives consolation!

The icon is the radiance of the Incarnation!

The Blessing of Icons

The Greek Euchologion gives only one prayer for the blessing of all icons. The Slavic Euchologion has several prayers for the different types of icons, those of the Lord, of the ever-Virgin Mother, and of the saints. I quote here only one of the Slavic prayers, and the Greek prayer. Both could be used for all types of icons. The ceremony is also a combination of both Slavic and Greek traditions. The icon to be blessed is exposed on a special stand in front of the Iconostasis with the sprinkler of holy water and the holy oil. The priest puts on his epitrachelion and his phelonion. He incenses around the icon saying:

P. Blessed is our God at all times, now and always and forever and ever.

R. Amen.

Glory to You. . . O heavenly King. . . All holy Trinity. . . Our Father. . . For thine is the Kingdom. . .

The owner of the icon, or the reader recites:

Psalm 89

I will sing of the mercies of the Lord . . .

Then the priest says the first prayer:

O Lord, Master of all, God of our fathers, Trinity glorified and worshiped by the whole creation, whom no one ever saw, we proclaim You and we confess that You are our God, a Father without beginning, a

Son equal to the Father, and a Spirit equal in honor and glory and worshiped with the Father and the Son. Thus we have learned from Holy Scripture and thus we believe.

In the Old Testament You have given us a symbol of Your Trinity in the three angels who appeared to Abraham; and in the fullness of time You showed Yourself to us in the face of the only Begotten Son, Our Lord and God Jesus Christ who was born of the ever virgin Mary, who was baptized in the Jordan river by John the Baptist, who was transfigured on Mount Tabor and who ascended into heaven on the Mount of Olives. You also sent upon us Your all Holy Spirit in the form of a dove and in the form of tongues of fire. You have taught us how to venerate Your image in the face of our Lord God and Savior Jesus Christ which He imprinted on the shawl which Abgar, the King of Edessa, had sent to him. With this picture the King and his people obtained great miracles of healing.

Since You accept and bless representations of Your Son and of Your Saints, deign to look favorably upon this icon which Your servants have prepared as an instrument to sing Your glory and to honor Your only Begotten Son, Our Lord and God Jesus Christ and his all holy Mother, the ever-virgin Mary, our Lady and Immaculate Queen of all.

(We also honor the memory of Your saint N... who is represented in this icon.)

Deign to bless it, to sanctify it, and to bestow upon it power for healing and forgiving sins. Let all those who pray to it with faith be heard and obtain Your special grace and blessing, and the tenderness of Your love, for You are our sanctification, and to you we send up glory, Father, Son and Holy Spirit, now and always and for ever and ever.

R. Amen.

The icon is sprinkled and baptized with holy water.

A Second Prayer

O Lord God, who have no beginning and no human form, Father of Our Lord God and Savior Jesus Christ, You have ordered Your servant Moses to draw a picture of the Cherubim made of wood, of gold, and of special embroidery, and to house it in the holy tabernacle, and later, in the temple of Solomon. We, Your servants, have received a similar order to draw holy icons in memory and honor of the appearance of Your Only Begotten Son in the flesh of our humanity which He has taken from the Holy Mother of God. We also draw holy icons in honor of Your saints who have pleased You and whose memory we venerate and whose lives we imitate.

We ask You, O Lord our King, hear our prayer and send down the grace of Your all holy Spirit and Your holy angels upon this icons. Sanctify it and grant it power of healing and purification. Let every one who prays to You in front of it be heard and his prayers be effective through the grace and mercy and tender love of Your Only Begotten Son with whom You are blessed with Your all Holy, good and life-giving Spirit, now and always and forever and ever.

R. Amen.

The priest seals the icon with the holy chrism from top to bottom and from left to right, saying:

Seal of the Holy Spirit. Amen.

And he concludes:

For You are the One who bless and who sanctify everything, O Christ our God, and to You we send up glory, and to Your Father who has no beginning, and to Your all Holy, good and life-giving Spirit, now and always and forever and ever.

R. Amen.

After the blessing the priest offers incense to the icon, prostrates himself before it and kisses it. All the people do the same while the special troparion of the icon is sung.
Let it be known that for the holy and divine Gospel book there is no blessing because it is the Word of God and real presence of our Lord and Savior Jesus Christ. It is sanctified and sanctifier. It does not need blessing. But the cover which is decorated with icons is blessed as icons are.

4. - The Temple of God

According to Saint Germanos of Constantinople the Church building represents "heaven upon earth, the place where the heavenly God resides and moves" (*Historia Ecclesiatica*). It is the house of the Incarnation of God where Christ our God acts upon us and sanctifies us, and where the transfigured world is gathered and organized in hierarchical order to be offered to God.

The walls and every corner of the building witness to the presence of God. The walls are covered with frescoes and icons. They mirror heaven by reflecting the angels and saints, the events of the life of Christ, of our Lady Theotokos, and of the Old Testament. The saints and angels in the frescoes and icons, and the faithful on earth, together form one family, "a chosen people, a royal priesthood, a consecrated nation, a people set apart to sing the praises of God" (1 Pet. 2,9).

In the Church the faithful are never isolated . They are surrounded and cuddled. They are visited and they visit. Unity with the saints and angels transcends time and space. Heaven and earth are joined to each other in a real and concrete communion.

As for the general disposition of the furniture in the church, it is strictly established. Icons, altar, vestments, liturgical books and every other object destined for the services are assigned to special places and their use regulated by a severe regimentation.

The Seventh Ecumenical Council of 787 declares that "even the composition of religious icons cannot be left to the will of the artist, but depends of the principles given by the Church authority and tradition. Only the art belongs by the Church authority and tradition. Only the art belongs to the painter, the ordinance and disposition belong to the Fathers."

The Russian Council of Stoglav, 1551, under Tzar Ivan IV and Metropolitan Marcarios of Moscow, dedicates a whole chapter (43) to the disposition of icons. What is important for us is the order given "not to paint except according to the image and resemblance of the ancient models left by our predecessors, the Greek Fathers." The artist has to conform not only to the iconographic prototype of the subjects he represents . . . but also to the place where each event represented is fixed and unchangeably determined. In entering the Church the faithful will thus find the same icons in the same place, as they would find the words of life in Holy Scripture in the same place.

DISPOSITION OF THE BUILDING

Our Christian church buildings have been modeled after the temple of Solomon which was built according to the plan shown to Moses on Mount Sinai. God himself is said to have indicated its general lines and disposition. The Church has not broken with the past. On the contrary, Christians have always believed that they were the inheritors of the Old Testament. Our churches are divided into three parts, according to the model given by God.

There is first the sanctuary, or the Holy of Holies, which is the most sacred part of the Church. It occupies the eastern side, and it faces east where the sun rises and light floods over the earth. The east symbolizes Christ who is "the Light of the world" and the "Sun of justice." It is also the place where the angels, the saints of heaven, and the just assemble to contemplate the luminous face of Christ.

On the opposite side there is the narthex, or vestibule, facing west, where the sun sets and light disappears. West symbolizes darkness, sadness, and the gloom of death. It is only after contemplating the beauty of the face of face west, to sanctify it, and fill it with happiness and goodness.

The Narthex is the place reserved for public sinners and catechumens, for penitents and those who have not yet joined the Church. From the narthex people are permitted to attend only a part of the holy services, which includes the proclamation of the holy and divine Gospel. In the narthex is also the baptismal font, and the fathers and monks appointed to hear confession and to forgive sins.

Between the sanctuary and the narthex is the nave, called also *ecclesia*, where the faithful stand to offer their worship to God. In front stand the cantors and readers and all clergy who do not take part in the services at the altar. The nave is in the form of a boat sailing toward the East, as if carrying the faithful towards the beauty of the face of Christ, toward light and life. Nave means, precisely, *boat* (navis), the ship of Noah, where salvation and security were found in the midst of deluge and destruction.

THE SANCTUARY

The sanctuary occupies the place of honor. It is on the eastern side. It is in the east where God is thought to be residing, where Christ lives and acts, where he awaits us, whence he comes to sanctify and sustain us in his grace and salvation.

Right in the middle of the sanctuary stands the holy table, the throne, where the God of our prayer and adoration reposes. We do not turn our backs to the east to conduct our prayers. We face the east, and we look up to God who resides there. On the holy table, as on a throne of glory, is the holy and divine Gospel book. The Gospel book is for us Christians the living Christ, the Word of God himself present in the word of man. Finally, it is on this same altar that the Son of God offers himself and the universe in the most awesome and most mysterious holy and divine

Liturgy. It is the table of sacrifice where Christ is immolated and yet alive.

The holy table is generally covered by two cloths, the first symbolizing the linen that wrapped the body of the Lord and the second representing the robe of glory of the risen Lord. On top of this cloth lays the *antimension*, called also *thronos* because, like a throne, it supports the Gospel Book of the Lord. It is unfolded only when the Anaphora is celebrated to support the Body and Blood of Christ.

On the left side of the altar stands the little table of preparation, or *Prothesis*, a simple table where the ministers prepare the oblations or elements for the sacrifice. It is here that the drama of Calvary starts unfolding. The office of Prothesis symbolizes the oblation of Christ which took place in his very Incarnation and was consummated on Golgotha. It commemorates Nazareth, Bethlehem, and Calvary, all important places where the Theotokos played an important role and where she takes an honorable place, a "queen standing at the right hand of Christ."

On or above the altar is suspended the Artophorion which contains the Body and Blood of our Lord and God in the consecrated Bread and Wine. This Artophorion is often in the form of a silver or a golden dove suspended from the ceiling, and extending to the middle of the altar. This symbolizesg the Holy Spirit who keeps the Lord Jesus Christ alive and always ready to feed the faithful. The Artophorion may be also in the form of a tabernacle. In front of the Artophorion, whatever shape it might be, there is always a candle or a lamp, flickering and alive, to indicate this special presence of Christ. These are the awesome mysteries that the Iconostasis protects and at the same time reveals.

At the very end of the sanctuary, right in the center of the apse, there is the Lady, the Mother of God "higher than the heavens" (*Platitera*). She holds in her arms the *Pantocrator*, the "One who holds the universe in his hand." Mary is conscious and proud of her Motherhood. She is sometimes seated and sometimes standing, but always in a sublime and peaceful attitude. Her oval face, with two large brown eyes, radiates serenity and grandeur. She is wrapped in imperial majesty. Her outer robe is like a cloud. Her court is composed of young maidens all dressed like Roman patricians, (as in the sixth century Church of Saint Appollinarius in Ravenna). Her court might be archangels in long flowing tunics, bowing respectfully to their queen and mistress. Her court might also be composed of the Fathers of the Church.

THE ICON-SCREEN

The Icon-Screen is not a wall of separation. It is rather a connecting link between heaven and earth, and a passage from earth to heaven. The Icon-Screen is the boundary line between time and eternity. According to St. Simeon of Thesalonika (1429): "The Icon-Screen indicates that behind it there is the sanctuary where Jesus Our Lord resides in his glory, surrounded by angels and saints" (*On the*

Holy Liturgy). The icon-screen displays icons of our Lord, of his mother, and of the saints and angels. It reveals that all separation has been overcome and that reconciliation has been achieved between God and humanity. God has descended to his beloved people - and his people can enter and ascend to their God.

Every face and every event painted on the Iconostasis points to and reveals the mysteries behind it, and leads us "by the hand" to the contemplation of the face of God. The Royal Doors indicate that the Lord will come to us as our Nourishment, Master, Judge, and Salvation.

THE DOORS

Along the length of the screen there are three openings, or doors: the one in the middle is called the Royal Doors; the one on the north side is dedicated to the Archangel Michael and is adorned with his icon; and one on the south side is dedicated to the Archangel Gabriel.

Michael is represented standing with a drawn sword, the defender and guardian of the gate of Eden, the first paradise. This door is also the service door, used by minor clerics and anyone who plays a role in the liturgical services. The door on the south side is painted with the icon of Archangel Gabriel. It is the door of deacons, leading to the sacristy or diakonikon, where the sacred vessels and vestments are kept.

Michael and Gabriel are also considered as deacons serving at the celebration of the Divine Liturgy. The icons of these two archangels are generally among the most beautiful in Byzantine iconography. Michael which means "who is like God," and Gabriel, which means "power of God," are the two principal representatives of the heavenly court. Each one holds the staff of a messenger (when Michael does not hold the sword) because they are, like all angels according to St. Paul, "serving spirits for those who shall inherit salvation" (Heb. 14).

The Royal Doors open in two directions, one wing to the left and one wing to the right, (whence the plural "doors"). The Royal Doors is the passage-way from earth to heaven, from this world to the world of the Kingdom of God; and in a return movement, from God to earth. Through the Royal Doors we have access to divine realities, to the Body and Blood of the Lord, whence divine realities come to nourish and save us. The Royal Doors is the sign of the Incarnation through which the Son of God came down to earth to dwell among us. It is a symbol of the invitation of God to the Kingdom.

Only the bishop, and clerics in full liturgical vestments, are allowed to pass through the Royal Doors. They are generally closed except for special movements during the holy and divine liturgy, and for very special liturgical occasions.

The upper half of the Royal Doors is painted with the Icon of the Annunciation. The scene depicts Mary pronouncing her acceptance to become Mother of God. The Holy Spirit, in the form of a dove, comes down from heaven to overshadow her and fill her with grace. He performs the miracle of Incarnation in her womb where the Son of God becomes really and truly present in our human flesh.

Often in the middle there is the scene of communion, the second real presence of God in a physical form. Christ gives his Apostles the Bread of his Body on one side, and the chalice of his Blood on the other. Sometimes this "incarnation" is represented by the so-called liturgical Fathers, those whose names are associated with the various forms of our Divine Liturgies.

On the bottom half of the Doors we may have the four Evangelists seated at their desks, busy writing their holy and divine Gospel books, which constitute the third real presence of the Lord. As the Holy Spirit has effected the first Incarnation of the Son of God who became Son of man in the womb of Mary, so also he is here overshadowing the Evangelists, effecting the Second Incarnation, a real presence where the Word of God becomes word of man, a Book. His Presence in the Book is no less a real presence, no less a precious reality of God among us, than his Presence in bread and wine.

THE HIGH-PRIEST

The two most important icons on the screen are, on the right side, the icon of our Lord, the High Priest, and on the left side, the blessed Mother of God, Queen of the universe and *Hodigitria*, she who points the Way.

In his icon, Christ holds his holy and divine Gospel book on his left side. His right hand gives the High Priestly blessing. The same gesture of the hand might also be calling for silence and attention to indicate that Christ is the only Interpreter, the only real Teacher of his word. His whole attitude radiates a sense of majesty and inspires confidence and security.

In this icon Christ the High Priest tells us never to be disturbed or frightened, because he is the Savior of all; he is the only One who presides over the destinies of this world. On either side of his head are placed the Greek letters *alpha* and *omega*, or the name of the Almighty God, *'o On*, "He Who is." This is the title of the Eternal, the beginning and the end of everything. He is the God of God, one with the Father and one with the Spirit. He is from all eternity and will remain for all eternity. This icon radiates divine character, and much tenderness and magnanimity. Power and serenity combine to tell us that Christ is our God and at the same time a real human being, like us. In some icons he is crowned with an imperial crown, to indicate that he is also the King of all, our King and our God. The tones of red and gold combined in the halo give the face an elegance and beauty that penetrate to our inmost hearts. Only a deep sigh will satisfy our faith in him: "You are our King and our God."

THE QUEEN

On the left side of the Royal Doors, the Theotokos, Mother of God, is enthroned in sublime majesty. She is the glorious Mother of God, and her title is written in red and gold on both sides of her head (*Miter Theou*) as if it were coming out of her halo, or perhaps a part of it. We must remember that in Byzantine iconography, Mary is never and cannot ever be represented by herself. Motherhood is a personal relationship, a relationship that binds two persons and identifies them as belonging to each other; one cannot be without the other. A mother is not a mother without a child, as the child cannot exist without a mother.

After the Council of Ephesus in the year 431, when the Fathers defined that Christ was as real a man as he was real God, Christian people and the whole church concluded that Mary was *Theotokos*, Mother of God, inseparable from her divine Son. In Eastern churches, Mary has always been and will always be represented visibly carrying her Son and God. Theotokos, Bearer of God, is her title to our devotion and veneration, and the whole raison d'etre of her being in our churches.

When we consider that Mary gave flesh to God, that she carried him in her womb, nurtured him, and accepted being his close partner in the redemption of humanity, our intellects as well as our imaginations are set on fire to discover some of the wonders God performed in her. Since she is Mother of God, all miracles of heaven and of earth can be found in her. She is higher in honor than the Cherubim and the Seraphim. She is a virgin and a mother. She died and yet lives for ever with her Son and her God.

Mary is often seated in sublime glory as a queen on a throne corresponding to the throne of her Son who is on the right side of the Royal doors. In her icon she reflects all the glory Christ pours upon her. Her posture imitates the posture of her Son, with the same position of hands and feet.

Mary holds Christ tenderly and points to him. She is *Hodigitria*, she leads the Way to Christ. In her arms the divine Lord blesses with one hand; with the other he holds his yet unrevealed Word in a folded scroll. Sometimes he is shown with one of his sandals unloosed, and the other well loosed, which John the Baptist, the "greatest ever to be born of a woman" (Math. 11, 11), according to our Lord himself, "was not worthy to stoop down and unloose" (Mark 1,7). The picture tells us that his Mother does not only unloose it, she can both loose it and unloose it; consequently, she is even greater than John, greater than any human person born of a woman.

Dark tones and contrasting colors against a warm gold background give this icon a great decorative power. Her Son's mantle is all red, the color of full divinity. Hers is only tinted with red, symbolizing that she is only a sharer in his divine character. Her undercape is of blue, symbol of her human nature.

THE THREE STARS

Every icon of Mary proclaims the deep Christian truth that her virginity is of a divine character and not merely a sign of an ascetical life. Her maternity was also of a divine character. No other woman could be sublime enough to combine the two. Only Mary, because she was the Mother of God, was able to possess them both. This combination of virginal maternity and fertile virginity is in no way a negation of the value of sexual love. It is rather its salvation from corruption and death. It is the sign of its transformation into a flame that will never fade, and of its final transfiguration into glory.

On Mary's forehead there is a star, a symbol of her present state of virginity combined with her motherhood: she is Virgin and Mother. On her right shoulder shines another star, a symbol of the virginity that was her's before motherhood; and on her left shoulder another, telling of her glorious virginity after motherhood. She has always been Virgin, and her virginity will last as long as her glorious maternity, that is for ever and ever. She is Mother, and at the same time Ever-Virgin.

Sometimes the icon of the Lord, High Priest and King, and that of Mary, Queen of the Universe, are decorated with thin metal plates, mostly of silver and gold. This *basma* covers only the background and the borders but leaves the face and hands in their reality of flesh. Christians covered icons only to make them more beautiful and more valuable, and sometimes as a help for unexpected financial hard times.

JOHN THE BAPTIST

On the left side of the icon of our Lord, the High Priest, stands the icon of John the Baptist, the greatest of all the prophets, the forerunner of Christ, and the summary of the whole Old Testament. As summary and representative of the Old Testament, he bows down to Christ and accepts him in the name of all past generations.

On the right of Mary, the Queen Mother, stands generally the icon of the patron saint of the church. The patron is there representing the whole community in perpetual adoration and constant prayer. On the rest of the panelling, we may find the icons of the great hierarchs, Saint Basil the Great, Saint John Chrysostom, Saint Gregory the Theologian, and sometimes Saint Athanasius of Alexandria, or other Fathers of the Church.

Immediately above the Royal Doors is the icon of the Mystical Supper, where our Lord instituted the holy and divine Eucharist of his Body and Blood. The icon shows us the moment when the Lord offers Holy Communion to his Apostles. On one side six Apostles. receive the holy bread; on the other side, six approach the divine cup, the two elements of communion which are obligatory in the Eastern church. This gesture of Christ giving his Body and Blood emphasizes and singles out his sacerdotal character: He is the only Priest and the only Mediator.

DEISIS

In larger icon screens the *Deisis*, or icon of intercession, is often placed above the icon of the Mystical Supper The word *deisis* means "prayer". The Theotokos and Saint John the Baptist, the one representing the Old Testament and the other the New, are standing in an attitude of humble supplication. In the middle is the Lord seated on a throne, or crucified. In both attitudes, enthroned or crucified, the Lord has become Savior of the universe. He combines majesty, fortitude, and unending love. The delicate features of his face are those of a noble and kingly character, deeply compassionate and peaceful. St. John Chrysostom exclaimed, "I look at Christ crucified, but I see the King of all."

On his right side stands his mother, who carries in her outstretched arms the whole of humanity and creation, offering them to her divine Son for salvation and redemption. On his left side, St. John bows his head in an attitude of humility, receiving and accepting in the name of all humanity and creation.

The Deisis is a scene full of grace and elegant dignity, with an immense sense of compassion and peaceful confidence.

On both sides of the Deisis runs a series of icons which represent either the twelve Apostles or the twelve major feast of the year. The major feasts of the church express the totality of the Christian teaching. They are the "pearls of the divine dogmas," as they were called by Patriarch Germanus.

Above the feasts are, sometimes, the prophets of the Old Testament, with open scrolls in their hands, on which are written texts from their prophecies concerning the Incarnation. They all show a movement toward the Theotokos seated in the middle and dividing them, half on her right and half on her left. They are all transported, as in a solemn procession, by an elan of eagerness toward the Theotokos who is the image and fulfillment of all their prophecies. This is called our Lady of the Sign.

From the Iconostasis radiates an immense attraction of indescribable holiness which leads us to silent adoration. We are plunged deep into an atmosphere of intimacy that draws us closer to the invisible, and brightens our vision of the transfigured world in Christ. Its significant and important liturgical role have inspired and stimulated most icon painters and artists, carvers and designers, to create the finest and most exquisite works of art, wherein their faith and their Christian vision shine in beauty.

When in the year 987 the envoys of Vladimir, King of the Rus in Kiev, want around the world in a search of the true religion, it was not the truth or goodness in Christianity that attracted them, but beauty - the beauty and splendor of holy icons, mosaics, frescoes, and liturgical ceremonies of the Great Church in Constantinople. On their return to Kiev, they reported to the King their final decision: "We did not know if we were in heaven or on earth for there is certainly no such splendor or beauty anywhere on earth. But this we know: that God was there, living and moving among his people."

THE ICON-SCREEN

It was late in the sixteenth century that the icon screen was organized in the fashion we have it today. But its origin goes back to the very beginning of Christianity. The famous byzantinist N. Pokrovsky finds its origin in the catacombs of Rome. He writes:

> "There were small chapels in the catacombs where the Liturgy was celebrated particularly during the persecutions where burials were more frequent. The sanctuary is either an apse, or an alcove, separated from the rest by a low railing (a primitive form of our iconostasis) of which traces can be seen in some catacombs. It is into this apse that the

sarcophagus of a martyr was placed, serving as an altar for the celebration of the Eucharist; this is the origin of the custom of placing the relics of a martyr either in the altar itself, or on the altar of the antimension . . ." (cited by L. Ouspensky, *Theology of the Icon*, p. 82).

The first Christians were already imbued with the idea of the awesomeness of God. They reproduced immediately in their churches the "veil of the temple" that separated the Holy of Holies from the rest of the Temple. Our Christian sanctuary is, indeed, more holy than the Holy of Holies because, as Saint John of Damascus says, "the Old Law and all that conformed to the Law, was but a shadow . . . of the service we have . . . , which is the very reality" (*Discourse on the Icon*, 2,23).

In the fourth or fifth century the Church in East and West built, in front of the veil, a balustrade, or ramp, the height of a man's chest, on which one could lean one's elbows. This ramp separated the officiating ministers from the participating faithful in the action of Christ on the altar. It emphasized the sacredness of the action and set the place apart as a sacred place.

Sometimes this ramp was made higher and constructed with twelve columns of silver, ivory, or gilded oak united by an architrave, or beam. This was to heighten the view that the sanctuary was, in the words of Saint Sophronius, "the place which reveals the Second Coming of the One enthroned upon it, who will come to judge both the living and the dead."

The twelve columns were in honor of the twelve Apostles "who will sit on twelve thrones to judge the twelve tribes of Israel" (Matt. 19, 28). The Eucharist is, precisely, both a presence of Christ and a journey of the Church into the Kingdom of the Age to come. The holy and divine Liturgy is, before everything else, the gathering of those who are to meet the One to come and enter into his bridal chamber.

Chrysostom and many early Fathers and writers testified to the existence of the veil and balustrade. Eusebius, the famous church historian of the fourth century, writes in his *Ecclesiastical History* that Constantine the Great built in the Church of the Apostles at Constantinople a sanctuary "enclosed by screens, or lattice work." He also describes the church at Tyre as having a majestic throne, and seats orderly arranged, and an altar which was "surrounded so that the multitude might not touch it, by a fence of wooden latticework delicately wrought with the craftsman's utmost skill."

Paul the Silentiary, secretary of Emperor Justinian, gives a detailed description of a magnificent balustrade in the Church of Hagia Sophia in Constantinople. It was decorated with arabesques and semiprecious stones, with silver screens connected to twisted columns, and supported by oval medalions painted with the icons of Christ, the Theotokos, the prophets, and the Apostles.

Constantine VII Porphyrogenitus (905-959) in his description of the Church of the Savior, built by Basil I in the Great Palace, has this to say about the screen that separated the altar from the nave: "The splendor and brilliance of this chapel cannot be believed by anyone who has not seen it, so great is the quantity of gold, silver, precious stones and pearls to be found massed within its walls ... The pavement is entirely of solid silver ... the walls, ... are also covered ... with the gleam of precious stones and pearls. As for the enclosure which shuts off the sanctuary, what riches are not gathered there! Its columns are of silver, so is the balustrade on which they rest; the architrave supported on their capitals is of pure gold and in every part loaded with what India can offer by way of treasure ..." (cited in Charles Diehl, *History of Byzantine Art*, Vol. II).

In the Western Church of Rome, because of barbarian invasions and the decline of art, the balustrade was reduced to a simple railing which was later called the "communion rail."

Since holy icons depict Christ and the events of his life, the saints, and angels, Christian people hung them on the balustrade of the sanctuary. In the year 874, after the victory of the Church over iconoclasm (the heresy that rejected the legitimacy and the use of icons) the balustrade became a very popular place for displaying them. By the fourteenth century, the whole screen was turned into a huge icon stand stretching the entire width of the sanctuary and reaching upward to quite a considerable height, sometimes even to the ceiling. By the sixteenth century, this screen was officially called *Iconostasis* and readily accepted as a necessary part of the Byzantine Church everywhere in the world.

Consequently, we can say, that the veil and the screen in front of the altar always existed in our church. But hanging icons on the screen and the official name, Iconostasis, did not come until later in history.

PSYCHOLOGICAL NECESSITY

The Iconostasis, and especially the veil of the sanctuary, are of great psychological importance: for the initiated faithful, it protects them from familiarity and the routine of daily contact; for the uninitiated and unbaptized, it protects them from curiosity and scandal. For the faithful, it is an artistic splendor that lights up the darkness of our human vision. For the others, it is a protection against skepticism, or the mockery of holy things. No inquiring eyes, no philosophical examination can ever appreciate our Christian mysteries.

For us Christians, the world of God presents itself to us in two ways, as a thing we own, or as a mystery we face. What we own we can manipulate and waste. It is there. What we face penetrates our very being. It is a presence. What we face is greater than we are. It is sublime. It inspires wonder and amazement. We are careful not to soil or spoil it. What we own is replaceable. It is a thing we see and handle, and before which we stand indifferent or bored. We stand in awe and wonder and radical amazement of what we face: We possess nothing; we are in communion.

Awe, wonder, and amazement are not passing emotions but sources of never-ending joy and surprise. They are insights into the divine, and into whatever surpasses our limited capacities of understanding. Mystery is, indeed, an inexhaustible abundance of life which we cannot express or possess. To be accepted, understood, and celebrated, mystery must first be protected from scrutiny; then and only then can it be discovered in its inner reality, and become a presence, an object of wonder and amazement.

The question of the divine and the supernatural is not "where" or "what" it is, but a question of how to penetrate the sham of routine, and how to expose the falsehood of familiarity.

The veil we spread before the holy things of our religion is a psychological necessity. It is a protective screen for the positive aspect of the sacred, a remedy for familiarity and boredom.

We enter the sacred only when we give up attempts to possess it as a thing. It is only when we humbly admit that the sacred is unique and beyond our reach that we can face it.

To see the ultimate preciousness of things and of persons we need the eyes of angels. The most precious realities are unseen; that which is not readily available to our caprice; that which is not at our disposal; that which we know we cannot possess.

The veil in front of our altars communicates the indwelling preciousness of the mysterious, the dignity of the sacred. It inspires. It is a pointer to something more precious which dwells beyond it.

What we cannot comprehend by physical contact, we become aware of through awe. Our sacraments probably become magical gestures, or drab, empty, and boring ceremonies because lengthy explanations created the impression that we possess them.

Awe is the realization that things and persons are not what they appear to be. They point to something still more sublime.

The divine and the sacred are always in danger of being submerged in anonymity by explanation and analysis, or by routine. To celebrate the sacred and fight anonymity, to contemplate the singularity and uniqueness of a person or of a thing, we have to wait for the revelation, and to be caught up in awe.

The divine character of things and of persons is easily lost due to excessive familiarity. Banality and triteness are by-products of familiarity.

One way to stop the deadening disease of familiarity and boredom is to veil the sacred. The Iconostasis literally "screens out" both curiosity and analysis. It supports our faith and fills our hearts with a nostalgic desire to fly on the wings of love and encounter the Beloved.

In the presence of the Iconostasis a quiet intuition stills our senses by its gentleness and draws us to a truth greater and more wonderful than we deserve or desire. We see clearly, using not the dark glass of our eyes, but the clear crystal of our essential humanity.

It gives me a special pleasure to quote from my book, *The Eyes of the Gospel*, what the movement of doors really means in the performance of the mysteries.

THE ROYAL DOORS

At the holy and divine liturgy a cry rises loud and clear: "The Doors! The Doors!" The Royal Doors are then closed and the curtain drawn shut. The opening and closing of doors are significant actions in man's life, a part of the ebb and flow of life. A great mystery lies in doors. They hide or reveal what is inside and keep the heart in suspense. They are symbols of privacy, of retreat, of the mind's escape into quietude, or into a sad secret struggle, or into a joyous encounter. 'Heaven without doors is not heaven,' say the mystics, 'it is a hallway.'

Closing a door may signify finality, or weakness, or a tragic happening of life. The closing of doors is a mystic act. The ministers and the gifts are now hidden from the world, and inaccessible to human inspection. Like Moses on Mount Sinai, all ministers are completely immersed in the vision and contemplation of a heavenly intercourse with God himself. 'No one can look at my face and stay alive,' said the Lord. It is regrettable that the closing of the doors at this moment has been marred and almost neglected in most churches. It is a lack of understanding and appreciation of the real meaning of the most awesome moment and action of our Christian religion!

The more secularized we become, the more our vision of the sacred and the holy becomes blurry, even blinded. The closing of the Doors and curtains is not setting apart the clergy as if in a special class, shunning the people from participation. Participation in the Mysteries cannot be realized by physical contact, but by words and gestures that create an inner vision and plunge the whole man into the reality of the invisible and the mysterious.

The sanctuary and altar have been, throughout the spiritual development of the Church, gradually hidden and separated, not by an ecclesiastical, bureaucratic mandate, but by the Christian sense of the sacred, by the real sense of the awesomeness of the mystery of God.

John Chrysostom and all the Fathers constantly call the altar the "Terrifying table," and the mystery of the altar "Terrifying Mysteries," "the terrifying sacrifice of the Body and Blood of Christ to which we have to approach with fear and trembling." This is sacred "terror" and not fear of the unknown. It is a mystic trembling in the presence of heaven: "Take off your shoes," said God, "for the place where you stand is holy" (Exodus 3, 5).

The shutting of the Doors and the keeping of the altar of sacrifice hidden from physical sight is not a hindrance. If anything, it is a forceful and revealing statement that there is a mystery, and that we cannot see or experience this mystery by physical contact. No human eyes or physical sight can penetrate it or comprehend it. Only love and the surge of the soul on the wings of faith can meet the Lord and God of all. "We celebrate the Mysteries with closed doors and keep out the uninitiated," says Chrysostom, "not that we are ashamed of our rites, but that many are still imperfectly prepared for them." The lines and colors of the Iconostasis purify the vision of the initiated and believers and help them penetrate into the invisible for the contemplation and adoration of the divine Mystery. The closed Doors are a sign and symbol of a distinction, not a separation.

There are here three completely different states of being and consequently three different roles to be played at the mystery of Christ: the ministers of the altar, Christ mysteriously present, and the people of God. The Holy Spirit acts on the ministers; Christ acts on the elements and the ministers act on the people. The ministers here do not represent the assembled congregation as they did in the first part of the celebration. They represent now the person of Christ, risen and offering his eternal worship in heaven. They are "in heaven" with Christ, all made alive by the Holy Spirit.

The people are awaiting the descent of the Holy Spirit upon the sacrificial elements and the descent of Christ himself into them. They are expecting the opening of the Doors and are looking forward to seeing heaven open to earth, deluging them with life, joy and salvation. Heaven is hidden from their eyes now. But the revelation will soon burst out at the opening of the Doors which will reveal the unknown in holy Communion.

Opening a door is an act as mystic as its closing. It gives a sense of moving into a new pattern of human life. Opening the Holy Doors includes the highest glimpse of heavenly gladness, reunion, reconciliation, bliss of lovers too long parted.

To see uniqueness is a splendor and a supreme thrill. Looking into the golden depths of the Iconostasis, we have but one single reaction: "This is indeed the House of God; indeed it is the gate of heaven."

Part Two - The Second Incarnation

The Word of God
Becomes Word of Man

5. - The Holy and Divine Gospel

For Christians, one of our greatest glories is to possess the Holy and divine Gospel of our Lord, God and Savior Jesus Christ. The Gospel is immediately and intimately connected with his first Incarnation where the Son of God became Son of man.

The Gospel explains the first Incarnation, brings it to our human consciousness and to our human experience in a way that we can understand; in other words continues to make the Incarnation present. The Gospel is the Second Incarnation where the Word of God, the *Logos*, became Word of man.

Indeed, the Gospel is the translation into human language and human experience of the life-giving Incarnate Son of God. The same Eternal Son of God, who was only announced in the Old Covenant, was incarnated into our human flesh in the New Covenant and is now with us, forever present in our human language.

HUMAN AND DIVINE

The Gospel is truly a Second Incarnation, both human and divine. It is human because it is composed of human words which describe actions and events of human life, and because it is expressed by human intelligence with all the human limitations of our words and expressions.

It is divine because it is God who speaks in it, God who acts and God who saves. Eastern theology is quite definite that the Trinity is at work in the Gospel. The Father speaks his divine Word; the Son is the Word of God; and the

Holy Spirit reveals him and allows us to hear him while he, Christ, remains mysteriously hidden. This is what the Lord promised his disciples would happen once he had ascended into heaven:

"I still have many things to say to you but they would be too much for you now. But when the Spirit of Truth comes He will lead you to the complete truth. . . Everything the Father has is mine; That is why I said: 'all He tells you will be taken from what is mine.'" (John 16,13)

The words of the Lord are Spirit and Truth; the words spoken about him are the means by which we are introduced to the most intimate aspect of his personality. "We drink the blood of Christ not only when we receive the chalice," said Origen, "but also when we read or hear his Gospel."

ACTION OF THE HOLY SPIRIT

However, all the importance that we attach to the holy and divine Gospel does not make our Christian religion a religion of a book, for the Gospel does not reproduce everything that Christ said and did. It is true that the Gospel is life and truth. But this is because of the Holy Spirit who illumines it with inspiration and sustains it by his personal presence, completing and making clear what Christ has initiated. It is the Holy Spirit who enlightens us in the Gospel so that we can understand Christ's life and translate it into theology and spirituality, into liturgy and the icon. It is the Holy Spirit who presents the Gospel to our consciousness, not as a manual of behavior, but as a mirror where we can contemplate the very face of our Savior, reproduce him faithfully in our lives, and witness to him before the world.

Before he departed from this world, Christ promised to send the Holy Spirit to remain with us, to remind us of what he had done and said, and to help us understand his truth. "The Holy Spirit, whom the Father will send in my name," he said, "will teach you everything and will call to your minds all that I have told you" (John 14,25).

The Holy Spirit caused the Incarnation of the Son of God in the womb of the Virgin Mary, and thus the Son of God became the Son of Man; so also this same Spirit "overshadowed" the Evangelists and led them to verbalize, in the best possible way, some of what Christ had done and said.

Thus the Word of God, the Logos, became the human word, a book. The very divinity entered again into this world in the actions and sounds and words of our humanity, and dwelt among us. Christ went up to heaven in his body, but he remains living with us in the words and events of his earthly life in the Gospel. For us who are living in time the Gospel book is necessary for remaining in contact with God. We need to hear his voice in the Gospel, just as we need to see his face in the icon, and eat his Body and drink his Blood.

Because we Christians believe that the Gospel Book contains Christ himself, alive and active, we never touch it without first bowing deeply and reverently kissing it. As emperors and kings are attired in clothing of gold and precious materials, the Gospel Book, which is the "vestment of Christ," our King and our God, is always covered and bound in silver, gold, and the most precious of materials. This is true even in the poorest Melkite churches - and in all other Byzantine churches in the world whether they be in the mountains, the deserts, or large cities, in the mighty Kremlin of the Tsars or in the humblest sanctuary of the Ukraine. Furniture may be of miserable quality, or even non-existent in our churches, but the Gospel Book is always bedecked with the finest lace, or velvet, if not in silver or gold or precious gems.

At the consecration of a bishop the holy and divine Gospel Book is opened and the written pages are placed on the head of the one consecrated during the prayer of consecration. This signifies and declares that it is Christ and the Holy Spirit, alive and operative in the Gospel, who are the real consecrators, as the prayer says: "It is not only the mere laying on of hands that consecrates, but the Holy Spirit," and Christ living in the Gospel. (First prayer of Consecration).

Because it represents and contains the living Christ, the holy and divine Gospel Book is also placed on the altars of our churches to show it is "God on his throne."

PRESENCE OF OUR LORD

Our church believes that in the Holy Eucharist, the real presence of Christ in the bread and wine is for eating and drinking only. It is reserved for this most mysterious and most glorious union with the Lord Jesus Christ. It cannot be looked upon or talked to; yet it is adored. The icon is for visiting and for person to person conversations because in the icon we see a human face and we encounter a human person. A face is for personal relation and personal dialogue.

The holy and divine Gospel Book is for the proclamation of the Word of God. It is for instruction, and for singing the voice of our Lord. It is, therefore, for parades also. When the ministers of the altar, priests and deacons, carry the Gospel Book in procession or 'on parade', they lift it up high above their heads with reverence and adoring awe, visible to all. The Gospel Book is never carried in any other fashion. It is Christ really present in his word and in the events of his life. When the Gospel Book is carried in procession, or in parades, a retinue of servers offer incense and surround it with lit candles. At its passage, people are invited to adore Christ. The bishop, priests, and deacons chant: "Come, let us worship Christ, our King and our God, and bow down before him. . ." Ministers and people bow also in reverence, and they sign themselves with the sign of the cross, expressing their acceptance of the great wisdom of God who ordained such a marvel of his presence.

As soon as the proclamation of the Gospel is to be announced the minister invites everyone to "stand" in order "to hear the proclamation of the Holy Gospel. . ." Then the whole congregation rises in an enthusiasm of expectation, and acclaims the Lord who is going to reveal himself. They all make a majestic sign of the cross, bowing profoundly and saying, "Glory to You, O Lord! Glory to You!"

As soon as the proclamation has ended, our enthusiasm rises again, and we repeat the same shout of joy, while bowing again and making the sign of the cross, saying once more: "Glory to You, O Lord! Glory to you!" St. John Chrysostom says: "When the Emperor has spoken, we all acclaim him by saying : 'Glory to You, O Lord!' But when our Lord speaks in his Gospel, our faith rises to enthusiasm, and we repeat the cry twice, saying: 'Glory to You, O Lord! Glory be to You!' We sing this acclamation not only after the Lord has spoken as we do for the emperor, but even before he speaks."

REVELATION OF THE TRINITY

Indeed, we believe that the Gospel is light and the announcer of life. When Christ communicates himself to us and pours himself out in human words and in the events of his life, he communicates life and divine light. He said: "I am the Life. . . I am the way. . . I am the Light. . ."

As the Lord Jesus is revealed in the Gospel, the Father and the Holy Spirit are revealed also. In the Old Testament, God the Father was revealed in an incomplete and fragmentary fashion. St. Paul says that the Old Testament is a "pale manifestation of what was coming: the reality is Christ" (Col. 2,17).

Revelation means rolling up the veil. Slowly, the curtains of the mystery of God were raised through book after book of the Old Testament, revealing little by little, more and more, the "Unknown God" who, at the appointed time, revealed himself fully in the face of Jesus Christ. The author of Hebrews explains that "God spoke to our Fathers in fragmentary and varied fashion through the Prophets. But in the final age, He has spoken to us in the Son" (Heb.1,11).

As God the Father is revealed in the Lord Jesus, so is the Holy Spirit also revealed. The Holy Spirit echoes his inspiration in every word of the Gospel: "The word of God is alive and active: it cuts like any double-edged sword, yet more finely; it can slip through the place where the soul is divided from the spirit; or the joints from the marrow" (Heb.4,12). The Holy Spirit brings our Lord to every ear that can hear and to every heart that can understand. It is the Holy Spirit who carries the sound of the voice of the Lord, like pure, lifegiving oxygen, to every cell of our bodies and inundates us with life, light, and security. He deposits the truth of the Lord deeply in our souls, and through this truth takes up his abode in our inmost places. The Holy Spirit, who becomes in the word of the Gospel the permanent Dweller in us, will unceasingly generate power and grace, impelling us to life and goodness. Our Fathers used to compare the sound coming out of the Gospel to the gentle rain, to the morning dew, and to the wind that blows in every direction. When the rain and the dew find their place in the ground, they nourish the earth and give it life and fecundity; and when the wind blows, it penetrates everything it touches. The words of Christ need no human philosophy to explain them and make them alive and life-giving. Christ knows the way to our minds and to our hearts, and the Holy Spirit, the Immortal One, is always there inspiring and explaining.

MESSAGE OF THE GOSPEL

The Words of the Gospel do not need any human interpretations. They penetrate us and inspire us by their own power and by the presence of the Holy Spirit. Father La Grange, founder of the Ecole Biblique in Jerusalem, and creator of modern exegesis, used to say: "All we can offer the Gospel, to help understand it, is to explain its grammar." It is evident that theologians, biblical exegetes, and historians may pool their knowledge to elucidate this grammar and the meaning of biblical literature, but their explanations cannot be valid unless they are in unison with the song sung by the Holy Spirit and the living tradition of the Church universal.

The explanations human beings give are always limited and conditioned by their own ideas. Human interpretations also emphasize practical and immediate success, the averting of calamities, or the attainment of whatever we are seeking at the moment.

However, Christ's ideas are all inspired by divinization. They are the distillation of all facts and of all realities; they furnish sustenance to life in all its infinite dimensions. Christ acts in the Gospel as the ultimate arbiter of evaluation and appreciation. He is the only one who can clarify and explain his message. He clarifies, deepens, and integrates everything on a divine plane. His whole activity is centered on our divinization, and his teaching is so awesome that we can only stand in admiration and let ourselves be soaked by his sublime message. His teaching reveals to little children what even aged scholars cannot fathom.

The mission of Christ on earth, as described by the Gospel, was to divinize and free the human being from all slavery, even the slavery of the law. Christ's message and his whole mission was to lead humanity to the realm of the Kingdom, to the freedom of the children of God, which is the freedom to love.

For Christ, to love is to be free. Poured forth from God, love participates in the freedom of God because it seeks the interest of God which is primarily the good of the community. The daring teaching of the Gospel on divinization, on love, and on freedom, is beyond human expectation and human interpretation.

FIRST MESSAGE: DIVINIZATION

The most divine of all the commandments, which no prophet or any founder of religion ever thought to utter, was spoken by our Lord in an easy, clear, and natural way. His commandment was not just to love the enemy, or to love the whole world, but to "love as I have loved." Christ's love had two characteristics: first to love without limit or condition; second, to love "until the end" (John 13, 1).

This is awesome!

According to the Gospel, the expression "until the end" means to the extreme limit of courage and generosity, to the point of giving his life not only for the salvation of the just and the friend, but also for the enemy and the criminal. "Until the end" means also that he loved throughout his whole life and to the very last minute to his life. Christ loved until his death. Before his last breath he forgave his executioners and the thief who was crucified with him. Such a love, such a commandment to love, cannot be bestowed or practiced except by a divine Being, or by those who have been divinized. Neither could such a teaching be produced by human intelligence. Only an infinite intelligence and an infinite love could be its origin.

The Lord is truly Divinity, and he wants his followers to be and to act divine. This kind of love, which has no limit or condition, is the only love that can set us free. And only in freedom are we able to fulfill all the laws joyously and spontaneously.

The freedom of the Christian is maintained and strengthened by the Holy Spirit who is the River of Living Water flowing in us, bathing every corner of our being and every aspect of our lives. Then all the laws of God, and every other law, appears not as an obligation but as a ladder to help us ascend to God. When we are free and in love, we gladly climb any ladder to see the face of our beloved God.

SECOND MESSAGE: HUMAN DIGNITY

The Gospel is not only the charter of love and freedom but also the herald of human value and dignity. The Lord Jesus never used abstract concepts like "human rights," or "human dignity." He always recognized human rights and human dignity by honoring people in a direct and concrete way. Whenever he encountered a human person he recognized the image of God. He immediately honored each person, showing respect and dignity. Christ looked upon the sinner with love. He treated the adulteress, the publican, and the thief exactly as he treated the faithful disciples and the just. His acceptance of the human person had no limit or any condition.

To Christ, all human persons were children of the same *Abba* who "causes his sun to rise on the evil and the good, and sends rain on the righteous and the unrighteous" equally, without discrimination" (Matt. 5, 45).

This is perfection - to love and to forgive like God himself: "Be ye, therefore, all perfect as your Father in heaven is perfect" (Matt. 5, 48).

Christ's standard for human behavior is that just as God creates and loves human persons, he also wants us to take care of each other and bring each other to the fullness of our potentialities. After Zacchaeus (the "small in stature") had been accepted by the Lord for what he was, a sinner, he felt as tall as the universe. He immediately proved how well-founded was the Lord's trust. He recognized his own dignity and human worth and offered to take care of others: "Look, Lord, I am going to give half my property to the poor, and if I have cheated anybody I will pay him back four times the amount" (Luke 19, 8).

The Lord himself recommended his own beloved mother to John: "This is your Mother!" And he recommended his beloved disciple to his Mother: "This is your Son!" The predominant idea of the Gospel is that just as we are all safe in God's care, so we should be safe in each other's care. Of all the holy books of the world only the Gospel presents God as a Being of wonder and beauty who fills the human person with an abundance of security and love as to become for other human beings a haven and a strength. The Lord asked, "Who was the real neighbor?"

among all the people who came upon the Jew who had fallen among thieves. The answer was, "He who took care of him," in other words, a hated Samaritan, an outcast. The final pronouncement of the Lord was, "Go, do likewise,": even if you are an outcast, if you take care of others, you are really a child of God.

THIRD MESSAGE: GOD IS SECURITY

The Gospel tells us that, in God, the impossible becomes a fact. When we enter into relation with God, our relation is with an *Abba*, a "Daddy." We belong to him as much as he belongs to us. We are his children.

In our human language the word *father* is a mere word, a name. Many are called "father" without having any real relation of love and life. But the word *Abba* is a relation of love and life. "*Abba* - Daddy," indicates a face that belongs to only one specific person. The face of a daddy shines and smiles and melts us into tenderness. There is only one face on earth we can look at and say "*Abba* - Daddy." In his Gospel, and in all the stories he told, Christ points to God as our *Abba*. He teaches us to look at his face and call him "our *Abba* who art in the heavens." Our Lord uses the plural form. In the singular form the word heaven means a specific place where the angels and saints live, move, and do the will of God, as in the petition "thy will be done on earth as it is in heaven." The word "heavens," in plural, means every place, every direction in which our face turns. There we encounter the face of *Abba*. Everywhere our eyes look they will open to see the radiance of his face.

This is daring and sublime! By commanding us to call God *Abba*, Christ teaches that we are in relation with forgiveness, with joy, and with an ever ready, ever present salvation. He constantly reminds us that we are products of a love beyond all human expression, the love of God, our *Abba*.

At such a teaching our hearts sing for triumph. We recognize that our dignity is greater than heaven and earth, more precious than all the miracles of the universe. Because of the teaching of the Gospel, we understand that *we* are the most sublime of all creation. In the voice of Christ, Wisdom - which is God himself - seems to be a "delighting game, ever at play. . . at play everywhere in the world, delighting to be with the sons of men" (Prov. 1, 30). "God unites only with gods," says Simeon the New Theologian. And Gregory Nazianzen gasps with delight: "Indeed, indeed, man is a game in the heart of God."

A message which does not carry first and foremost a shock, a poem, something from the heart, is a message betrayed and condemned to be sterile. Every truth uttered by Jesus Christ is a truth that conveys life and joy because it has first been warmed in the heat of his love. Every gesture of Christ is a message and a poem that makes us sing "Glory!" Everything Christ did is designed to make our life a celebration. The message of the Gospel is filled with wonder, and every one of the events of the life of Christ contains a surprise of wonder and joy. The words of Christ are a life-stirring experience, allowing us to enter life and live it fully. Christ's voice in the Gospel is an ecstasy beyond and above any voice ever heard on earth. It penetrates our hearts and sweeps away ugliness and sin. The voice of Christ is the bearer of a sublime message which sings that we are on the road to another, livelier world, tinted with unimaginable wonders, alive with ultimate music, and bursting with radiance.

6. - Proclamation of the Gospel Message

The message of the Gospel is so awesome that our Church does not dare proclaim it without first expressing a challenge and a warning to the faithful. The challenge is to be fully awake and ready; and the warning is that the message is the greatest adventure a human being can ever face. Away with fear, hesitation and any other cowardice! "Let us pray to the Lord our God that we may made worthy to hear the proclamation of the holy Gospel..."

Shine in our hearts, Master who love mankind, the pure light of Your divine knowledge, and open the eyes of our minds that we may understand the announcing of Your Good News; set in us the fear of Your blessed commandments, so that trampling all carnal desires, we may begin to live according to the Spirit, both willing and doing everything for Your pleasure. For You are the light of our souls and bodies, Christ God, and we render glory to You, and to Your eternal Father and to Your all-holy, good and life-giving Spirit, now and always and forever and ever.

Since the message of the Gospel is a wondrous proclamation, it must be conveyed in a special manner. It must be intoned or sung, not simply read. For centuries, in East and West, it was always chanted and sung. In the Melkite Patriarchates of Antioch, Jerusalem and Alexandria, a special minister, called the "deacon of the Gospel," was chosen for such a service. Gifted musicians, and those endowed with artistic ability in reading, were invited, and they were the only ones allowed to proclaim the Gospel to the gathered church. The proclamation of the Gospel is a very special act of faith by which we convey the meaning of

Proclamation of the Gospel Message

the presence of God, Father-Son-Spirit, in whom we deeply believe, and to whom we commit our whole being.

The ancients, with a profound sense of wisdom, insisted on the way the voice should be modulated, the way the words should be pronounced, and the way the whole meaning should be brought out. Simple proclamation differs only a little from the spoken word. The proclamation of the Gospel should be characterized by a pleasant tone of voice, gentle inflection, and clear rendering of the meaning of the Word. Whether elaborate or simple, the proclamation of the Gospel must have this one characteristic: to convey the poetry of the text, and to create in people the feeling of glory and joy at being in the presence of God. Not everyone is capable of performing this function.

In our modern Church (as it was at the time of fervor and enthusiasm) a special training program in proclamation is given to clerics, and offered especially to those who are endowed with artistic ability of voice.

As the priest is the bishop's assistant in consecrating the Holy Eucharist, so the deacon is the priest's and bishop's voice in announcing the Gospel. The bishop's status in the church is supreme because the bishop is "maker" of the Eucharist. The priest's status is major because the priest is the assistant of the bishop in making and realizing the presence of Christ in the Eucharist. The deacon's status is also a major order in the Church because his main role is to proclaim the message of the Gospel and thus make Christ present in the hearts and in the thoughts of his people.

PEOPLE'S ATTITUDE

When the deacon or priest proceeds to the solea to proclaim the holy and divine Gospel, candles are lit around him. As far back as the fourth century, St. Jerome mentions this custom with admiration: "Whenever the Gospel is read, the Eastern churches light candles, partly to demonstrate their joy because of the good news which the Gospel brings, and partly as a tangible way of representing the light of which the psalmist speaks: 'Your word is a lamp to my feet and a light unto my paths'" (*Cant. Vigilant, III*).

People also stand. St. John Chrysostom remarks: "If the letters of a king are read with great silence, much more ought we to compose ourselves and stand up with attentive ears when the letters, not of an earthly king, but of the Lord of the Angels, are read to us " (*Hom. I on Matt*). Long before Chrysostom, the *Apostolic Constitutions* stated that "When the Gospel is read, let the priest and deacons and all the people stand with a profound silence" (II, VII).

When the Book is brought to the solea, all the people leave their places wherever they may happen to be, advance towards the Book, and surround it. All the concelebrants who are at the altar, come through the side doors of the Icon screen and stand with fervent attention on guard, facing the Gospel Book. The sick and the afflicted come still closer to the "physician of our souls and bodies."

In the Melkite tradition there is often a delegate from the congregation, a man or woman of special standing and dignity who, in the name of all, holds the Gospel Book on his or her bowed head as a sign of accepting, in the name of all, the presence of the Lord, his message and his love.

At the end of every paragraph sung by the minister of the Gospel, the whole congregation vibrates with the last sounding note. Everyone hums audibly the last word chanted by the minister, thus allowing time for the singer to rest, for the words to sink in, for the meaning to unfold, and for our admiration and enthusiasm to sigh. The hum demon- strates also that our acceptance of what is being said goes through our whole being and makes us vibrate with its life.

On some occasions the priest holds the open Gospel book for the bishop, and the deacon for the priest, but always on a bowed head, never on lowered hands. People from the congregation raise their hands to the level of the Gospel Book, or rest them on whoever is holding the Gospel Book.

Some Byzantine churches have a special decorated stand set aside only for the Gospel Book. Those who have been close to the Gospel Book, and those who have touched it, offer a special veneration to Christ by kissing the Book once the proclamation has ended. Each one then returns to his or her place in the church.

THE MINISTERS' ATTITUDE

The holy monk Isidore of Pelusium in Egypt mentions another custom which is still faithfully followed by ecclesiastics and dignitaries of the Eastern Church: "When the true Shepherd appears at the opening of the Holy Gospels, then the bishop himself rises and lays aside all symbols of his dignity or authority, signifying thereby that the Lord himself, the Author of the pastoral function, his God and his Master, is present".

At the proclamation of the Gospel bishops take off their crowns, put aside their staffs and all signs of power. The Lord is their dignity and their power.

The proclamation of the Holy Gospel is not only the manifestation of the Kingdom, but also its realization in the now of the community. At the office of matins, which is the celebration of a new day and the beginning of a new life, when the Gospel is to be announced, all the bells of the church peal their joyous and triumphant sounds, as if to say, "The Lord is here! Parousia is being made present! The Kingdom is at hand! The Eternal is over-flowing from out of his eternity to be alive in our measured time. The *Kairos* is conquering the pessimistic uncertainty of this world to make us share in the certainty of his own eternity."

Gospel readings are often introduced by the phrase "at that time," which is a guidepost to the opening of new horizons. This signifies that Christ is the *Kairos* of God, the moment of eternity eternally present. It is the time of Christ which happened two thousand years ago, but which is valid and real in the now. Christ is always present, always real, always carrying eternity to us and carrying us into eternity, and towards our final destination.

We shall rediscover the right attitude of worship and awe for the Lord, a living faith in him, bright enthusiasm for his teaching, when we rediscover the meaning of all these gestures and signs of adoration which Christian tradition has engendered to keep us watchful and alert. These ceremonies are the fruit of intuition enlightened by the living inspiration of the Holy Spirit, and they are richer and more powerful than any deduction of human logic and analysis. Followed with a reverent attitude, they bring the reality of the words of Christ and the events of his life to our consciousness.

VISION OF THE GOSPEL

The human race taught the Lord our God how to be human. The Gospel says, "And the child grew in age and waxed strong in spirit, filled with wisdom" (Luke 2, 40). But the Lord our God who became man taught humanity how to be divine, how to live and act and love like God, in the way that is proper to God. The basis for this new direction of life is the fact of our union with him. Its goal is to keep us united with him and with every human face on earth. The object of the whole teaching of the Gospel is union with God and union with others because we are children of the Kingdom, sharing in God's own life.

So, in a world of hatred, discord, and discrimination, Christ speaks of love, unity, and forgiveness without limit or condition: "Be ye all perfect as your Father in heaven is perfect" (Math. 5,48). This recommendation of the Lord Jesus sounds unreal and impossible. For our human minds, it is indeed unreal and impossible. But the Lord keeps on playing, in his divine way the game of the unreal and the impossible, in order to make it as real and natural as growing is for a child, because we are indeed children of his Kingdom. With the Holy Spirit we can make real even the unimaginable.

One pursues a vision with happiness and courage because one is attracted by its life-giving reality and inspired by its beauty. It is the last step that counts in reaching a vision. The last step for us Christians is in the Holy Spirit, and it belongs to him to lead us to live God's life.

Because he is God and the Lover of every human person in this world - *Philanthropos* - Christ is never negative or threatening in his Gospel. He does not deal with obligations. Love cannot be an obligation. Love cannot be negative or a threat. Love is a response to a personal revelation. Love is strong and always positive. If Christ ever speaks of the observance of law, of punishment or reward, he does so only to relate to people where they are, and uses thought patterns familiar to them. But in the process he always raises the level of their thinking, and redirects it towards pure love. He changes the whole perspective of our humanity into a divine vision.

Buddha, Confucius, Moses, and the Prophets gave the world the strictest commandments and the most beautiful codes of behavior, but they always attached them to rewards or punishments. The Prophet Mohammed added to all this a marvelous legal system built on logic and the rules of behavior. Every one of their laws, commandments, and social rules came from logic and were connected with threats of punishment, or hope of reward. But the Lord's commandment in the Gospel is to be a disciple, to follow the example of the Master and identify with him.

BEATITUDES AND DISCIPLESHIP

Law aims at doing something, while discipleship aims at being someone special. Being the disciple of Christ means acquiring his vision and his attitudes towards life and towards people. Law seeks to please. A disciple seeks union of mind and heart in order to grow in love as the Lord has loved "Go, therefore, and make disciples of all the nations" (Matt. 28, 19). He did not say to make them law abiding! Our Lord re-wrote all the laws in order to make them a revelation of God and an invitation to share in his divine life. The code our Lord gave the world came from his heart and from the abundance of his love. He gave us Beatitudes, divine dreams, divine aspirations, - not laws.

The Beatitudes are like magic carpets which transport us to the open vistas of the unbelievable splendors of life. They keep us in tune with the hope that someday we will fully live our divinization and discipleship. Each one of them is as vast as the universe; yet, each can be fitted neatly to every man and woman's size and measure. Each one is an open door that invites; but no one can enter unless he or she is burning with an inner flame, and ready for a continuous struggle with the world of selfishness, violence, and injustice. The Lord meant the Beatitudes to be the one and only necessary charter for social and religious life. He invites us all to his table - the lame, the blind, the poor, the sinner, the just: "If you want to be perfect, go, sell your possessions and give it to the poor, and then come and follow me" (Matt. 19, 21); "If anyone will follow me, let him deny himself first . . . (Mark 8, 34).

The Beatitudes are so sublime a charter that the Church commands us to sing and repeat them throughout the whole year on every single Sunday of the year, when the whole community gathers for the Eucharist.

Sunday is the day of the proclamation of the Beatitudes, as it is the day for the proclamation of the Resurrection. Chrysostom says: "The Lord Jesus does not introduce what he says by way of advice or by way of commandment, but by way of a blessing, so as to make his word and teaching less burdensome, and to open to everyone the course of his discipleship. He did not say 'this or that person,' but 'they who do so, all of them, are blessed.' So, though you be a slave, a beggar in poverty, a stranger, unlearned, there is nothing to hinder you from being blessed, if you emulate the beatitudes" (*Com. on the Beatitudes*).

> *Blessed are those who have the spirit of openness,*
> *for the Kingdom of God belongs to them.*
> *Blessed are the non-violent,*
> *for they shall possess the earth.*
> *Blessed are those who cry for compassion,*
> *for they shall be consoled.*
> *Blessed are those who hunger and thirst for holiness,*
> *for they shall be satisfied.*
> *Blessed are the merciful,*
> *for they shall obtain mercy.*
> *Blessed are the pure of heart,*
> *for they shall see God.*
> *Blessed are those who work for peace,*
> *for they shall be called children of God.*
> *Blessed are those who are persecuted for justice' sake*
> *for the Kingdom of God is all theirs.*

LEARNING THE GOSPEL

The Gospel cannot possibly be a book for study only. Every pronouncement of the Lord is a miracle of beauty that is beyond our human analysis and expectation. One can enter into its limelight only by an unselfish surrender and a generous disposition of heart. It is not study, but standing in admiration and awe before every act, word, and event of the life of our Lord that will make us understand. The Gospel must be proclaimed and chanted to allow every ear that hears vibrate with its sound, and every heart that can understand be soaked by its warmth.

The Gospel is not a teaching, but a proclamation of something unbelievably divine. It is about how to live the life of God. We are not just creatures, says the Lord, but sons with the Son. We have been made divine. The life we live now is not our own, for Christ lives in us. We are called to live not on our level, but on God's level, which is the level of divinization.

To live the life of Christ involves taking on the attitudes and values of Christ, the attitudes and values he expressed in the Beatitudes. Loving as he has loved is beyond the natural range of our intellect and the power of our wills. We lack the generosity to do this; we cannot even conceive of what it is. What the Lord is and what he has to say goes beyond the intelligence and power of any created being. The whole community must be involved and absorbed by it. It has to be proclaimed in the community and for the community. The Gospel cannot be a personal study.

The Gospel is Christ himself speaking, singing, playing his divine games. Its proclamation must be surrounded with beautiful ceremonies to awaken in us the sense of the luminous and to allow us to be ready to accept the invitation of Christ to partake of his supper and to enter his Kingdom.

7. - The Gospel in the Liturgy

The liturgy distributes the four Gospels throughout the four seasons of the year, one Gospel for each season. In the spring the Gospel of St. John proclaims that the Christian is a Christophore, or carrier of Christ. In the summer the Gospel of St. Matthew calls the Christian to be a pneumatophore, or bearer of the Spirit. In the fall St. Luke preaches how to be a paterophore, or bearer of the Father. And in the winter St. Mark's message concerns the Christian as a somatophore, or care-taker of the good order of the universe, and especially a care-taker of one's own body.

In the first three seasons Christians contemplate life in the light of the Persons of the Most Holy Trinity in order to understand their own lives and their vocation to divinization, which is to live the life of God by being disciples and followers of Jesus Christ. In the last season they learn how to be care-takers of nature and of their own bodies in order to return them to the state of paradise. Christians are called to recreate paradise.

SUNDAY

The Sundays of the year are different from other days. Sunday is the day of the Lord, the *kyriake*, the day that presents presents the person of the Risen Lord whom we meet, honour, and greet with affectionate fellowship. We approach Sunday as if we were entering the bridal chamber of the Bridegroom.

During the Easter season the other six days of the week are an extention of Sunday. It is the first of the week, the fountainhead of inspiration and courage because it is

Christ himself who will carry us, as on his own shoulders, throughout the days of the week, he who is the life, light, and the sustenance of our pilgrimage. Christ is, indeed, the bright cloud "who walked before the people of Israel to lead them through the desert to the "promised land." That is also why, during the forty days of Easter, we do not fast or abstain or do penance, because we are carried by Christ who is our holiness and our salvation.

After the Ascension of the Lord and the descent of the Holy Spirit on Pentecost, Sunday becomes the end of the week and its last day. The days of the week are like a great procession and a pilgrimage to meet Christ and rest in Him. During the six days of the week we may fall into sin, we may cry over our shortcomings, we may be in pain and suffer, yet our eyes are focussed on Sunday where Christ will be our repose and our salvation. We revel in him. We feast playfully and enjoy him who is joy and our security. During the week we fast and abstain and do penance, yet we are sure to find full forgiveness in Christ. The days of the week are only a pilgrimage, or a parade, to Sunday, where the Bridegroom awaits us to repair any damage we might have sustained, and restore us to health and happiness.

Our Melkite mothers and fathers were always aglow with delight when they talked about Sunday. For them, Sunday was the day of the Bridegroom waiting for our affection, and for whom flowers and perfumes were strewn all around the house. For the Bridegroom we donned our best robes, and in his honour the best food awaited the whole family. Sunday was the radiance of the beauty of the face of Christ in which we could see, like in a mirror, each other's face.

Through the seventy years of my life I am still aflame with wonder and amazement as I remember the story told me as a child about the light that shines on Sunday. Our ancestors believed that the light that brightens Sunday is unlike the light that comes out of the sun, moon or stars. It is the very special light God had created from the beginning of the world to light up paradise. When Adam and Eve sinned and

Paradise was lost, God hid its light in heaven and reserved it only to the angels. But when Christ rose from the dead and Sunday became the day of the encounter with Christ, God released it again upon the earth to illumine Sunday and make us able to see the face of Christ and every human face. In this light every face becomes aglow with loveliness. For this reason our Melkite people keep the doors of their homes wide open on Sunday to receive visitors and to pay visits to each other.

THE OCTOECHOS

In honor of Sunday the Church has composed a special hymnal, an epic poem in which our tongue and intelligence and soul seem to be trembling with excitement and delight. Gladness and joy are the two main words repeated again and again in every hymn of the poem. Happiness and security in God are the theme constantly repeated to express and evoke joy in the very recesses of our being. Repetition is a psychological method intended to move us to goodness, freedom, truth and wisdom.

This hymnal book is called the *Octoechos* which means eight tones. The science of music discovered that the voices and sounds of the universe and all human music, could only vibrate in one of these tones.

The Christian Church sings the beauty of the face of Christ in all the eight tones. Every Sunday, and every day of the week that preceeds or follows Sunday, the universe hears the Christian sing Christ in one of these tones, and the Christian hears the universe sing with him the joy of his Christ. All the eight tones are thus repeated through the year, Sunday after Sunday and week after week. They will be sung as long as the Church will last and as long as the Christian can sing.

The *Octoechos* was composed by a Melkite, St. John of Damascus. Its poetry warms the heart, creates radiance, and gives meaning to life, death, and resurrection. It celebrates a celestial brightness which somehow brings us nearer to the enduring brilliance of God. Its hymns are short, repetitive, and their rapidity transforms our religious experience into exalted joy where we are at the mercy of Christ alone and where the blows of fate are warded off.

The troparia constantly repeat the theme that everything in heaven and on earth and under the earth is soaked with the reality of God, a reality of life, light, and the joy of living. Every troparion is marvelously constructed, step by step, carefully building each new element upon the former. They are masterpieces of structure and balance. Every piece is composed and developed skillfully, repeating the same theme over and over again. A little variation is added each time, and it is the variation and the constant repetition of the same idea that created a vibrant and intense emotion. St. John of Damascus is the lyre of the Spirit.

All this music, all the greetings, flowers, and perfumes, are still insufficient to express the whole longing that is in the heart of the Christian. Sunday cries out for more intimate companionship with the Bridegroom. It thirsts for the Holy Eucharist, our Bridegroom, who opens his bridal chamber to receive his beloved one. He is the Spouse to whom we are engaged and for whom we sing out our joy. On Sunday we encounter a Divine Person with whom we experience harmony and unity. On Sunday we encounter Christ, not as an external norm of conduct, but as a Bridegroom who loves and whom we love in return.

CYCLE OF ST JOHN

The Gospel of Saint John is the Gospel best suited to give a clear picture of Christ as real-man, real-God, and to explain the Christian call to divinization. The spring is entirely dedicated to the proclamation of St. John's Gospel.

Spring is the time of new life, new hope, and new vision. Nature wakes up and is renewed. Christ rises from the dead and gives new impetus to mankind and to creation. During this time Christians contemplate Christ, his Person, his work, and the new direction of life he gives to humanity. "We become what we contemplate," the Fathers say. Because we contemplate Christ we become Christophores.

The proclamation of John's Gospel extends from the day of the Resurrection to the day of Pentecost, the descent of the Holy Spirit. During this whole period the general message is one of celebration. It is the time of joy and triumph. During this period we constantly sing the hymn of the Resurrection, *Christ is risen!* Life is given! Christ has conquered by blotting out every sin and saving every sinner. He is alive and real among us, and we are one with him. As long as this period lasts we do not do penance. We do not kneel in sorrow for our sins. We do not fast or abstain either. We are identified with Christ who is our forgiveness and our salvation.

The Gospel proclaimed on the day of Resurrection at the holy and Divine Liturgy is not that of the story of resurrection but the story of our divinization. We are carried to the eternity of God. We proclaim with St. John that our origin was in the heart of God, that now we live in the heart of God in the risen Lord, and that our destiny is going back to the heart of God with Christ:

> *In the beginning was the Word...*
> *and the Word was God,...*
> *Through whom all things were made*
> *and without whom was made nothing*
> *of what was made ....*

John's Gospel is the last of the Gospels in time of composition but first in importance. Origen has this to say about it: "I think that just as the four Gospels are the foundation of the faith of the Church - and on these foundations rests the entire world reconciled with God in Christ - so too the Gospel according to St. John is the principal Gospel, and no one can seize its meaning, who has not leaned on Jesus' bosom, does not have Mary for his mother" (*Prologue of the Commentary on the Gospel of St. John*, quoted by Ouspensky-Lossky, *The Meaning of Icons*, p. 113).

The main idea of St. John's Gospel is that, if the Word was made flesh, it was to give life and salvation to the world, and to make us children of God.

Sunday after Sunday, day after day, all during Easter time, the Gospel of St. John tells us about the person of the Lord. The Lord Jesus is indeed a being from heaven, yet he is entirely human. He is humble and simple, even in his risen glory. All the historical events of his life are at once both human and divine, historical, yet rooted in eternity. The miracles are signs which manifest Christ's glory; they are symbols of much greater realities. According to John, Jesus Christ came to be

> the Light of the world,
> the Bread of life,
> the Living Water,
> the perfect Shepherd,
> the true Vine.

His Body is the temple of God which will rise in glory even after it has been destroyed and he has died.

In order to understand Christ and witness to him in our own lives, we must wait for the Holy Spirit who will speak clearly and explain all that Christ has done and said. Thus, Christians who have contemplated Christ and lived his divine person will become Christophores, Christ-bearers.

CYCLE OF SAINT MATTHEW

Summer follows spring. After the Resurrection and Ascension of the Lord the Holy Spirit comes at Pentecost. Like summer, the Holy Spirit is sun-shine, growth, and maturity. The Christian who became Christophore at Easter time has to become Pneumatophore, bearer of the Spirit and witness of the vocation to divinization.

Development and growth is a long process, so the cycle of Saint Matthew is the longest of all the Gospel cycles. It lasts eighteen weeks. Week after week and Sunday after Sunday, the message is impressive and repetitive. Christ's teaching and ideals are sung and proclaimed with persistance every day. The Holy Spirit is continually invoked to enlighten and strengthen us in all the struggles we encounter for the sake of the Kingdom.

Saint Matthew is the best teacher because for him Christ is the Teacher par excellence, far superior to the Scribes, Pharisees, or any other teacher. Saint Matthew's Gospel is a handbook of Christian conduct to be used by all teachers.

The most important message of Saint Matthew is that Christ is the real Messiah who came to bring the Law and the Prophets to to perfection, not to destroy or diminish them. He comes also to remove their onerous burdens and blind alleys. As Master and Lord, he reduced them to one commandment alone, that of love, which is freedom. For Christ, to love is to be free, and to be really free is to love. Poured forth from God, love participates in the freedom of God because it seeks the interest of God which is primarily the good of the community.

Another very special teaching reported by Matthew (that no one else dared to report) is that "those who take the sword shall perish by the sword" (Matt. 26, 52). The Kingdom of God does not come about through brute force or physical violence, but by the practice of the Beatitudes.

St. Matthew insists that the Lord Jesus is the friend of the poor because he is one of them. He renounces wealth and power and orders his disciples to do the same. Finally, the Lord Jesus is the "Son of man" whose saving work is accomplished through his passion and death, and manifested in his glorious Resurrection.

The Christian who learns these lessons of the Lord, and tries to live by them, is a Pneumatophore, a bearer of the Spirit.

CYCLE OF SAINT LUKE

After the steady growth and maturity of nature in summer comes the time of the harvest. Nature gives of her boun-ties, and man gathers all that he will need for his sustenance. It is time for the Christian to enter into the life of the Father and become a Paterophore, a bearer of the Father. Luke stresses his Master's love of sinners and records many instances of forgiveness, of Christ's tenderness for the lowly and the poor. Also, St. Luke shows Christ's severity toward the proud and toward those who abuse their wealth. Another lesson we gather from Saint Luke, which Matthew and Mark did not mention, is joy in God and gratitude for his gifts.

Sunday after Sunday the Church reads these episodes at the holy and Divine Liturgy in order to reproduce these attitudes of Christ in our lives so that we may become one with the Father - Paterophores.

Lastly, Luke insists on the necessity of prayer (for which the Lord Jesus sets the example), on repentance, and on the treatment of self with unflinching detachment, especially from riches. Thus we are led into the period of Lent and the cycle of Saint Mark.

CYCLE OF SAINT MARK

It is now winter time, a period of introspection and self-examination. Christians reflect on their own needs and the needs of others. Christians have a physical dimension; they are somatophores, with passions and desires to tame and channel. Fast, abstinence, acts of penance, and bodily exercises will help us overcome the difficulties of life and follow Christ.

Mark highlights the difficulties the Lord himself encountered in his life. The general public received the Lord Jesus warmly at first; but their enthusiasm waned as they found that his gentle, other-worldly conception of the Messiah did not fulfill their expectations. Yet, even rejected and crucified, Christ remains the Messiah and triumphant Envoy of God. Our Lord is really Son of God, acknowledged as such by the Father, by the devils, and by humanity. He is of divine rank, and higher than the angels. The mockery, the rejection by the public, the antagonism of the Jewish leaders, even the lack of understanding of his disciples are some of the many hostile activities that Mark tries to explain. For Mark, the Cross was God's mysterious plan to redeem the world, and this plan was vindicated in the glory of the Resurrection of Christ.

In his miracles the Lord Jesus always asks for discretion and silence because he wants to prevent an ill-advised enthusiasm in the crowds who were seeking a worldly Messiah. He calls himself "Son of Man" as a cautionary measure, to avoid minunderstanding and false hopes for any political involvement.

In the cycle of Mark the somatophore Christian becomes refreshed, stronger to face the great and Holy Week, more ready to rise again with Christ in his Resurrection.

GOSPELS IN HOLY WEEK

The holy and Great Week of the passion of our Lord is a majestic unfolding of the whole work of Redemption. During the services of this week the four Evangelists intermingle in long and detailed narrations of the last days of the life of the Lord, of his suffering and death. The same episode may start in Matthew; it is repeated again and again in the words of Mark and Luke and may end with John's final description. The same episode may also be reversed. It may start in John only to re-echo in Luke or Mark and end in Matthew. All four Evangelists harmonize. They all witness to the reality of our salvation. They describe the journey of God with our humanity, and the glory of the final triumph of Resurrection.

The holy week services allow the Old Testament (which is but a preparation and herald of the Gospels) to mingle in the episodes of the life of Christ. Long selections are read to demonstrate that all the expectations, dreams, and hopes of the whole history of mankind have been fulfilled in Christ. Christ is the focal point and final realization of every longing of the human heart.

THE EVANGELISTS IN ICONOGRAPHY

In iconography the Evangelists are generally represented seated before a lectern, reading or writing the first lines of their respective Gospels. They also may be indicated by the *tetramorph*, or the four mysterious representations announced by Ezekiel, the prophet: "Out of the midst of fire ... and brightness ... came the likeness of four living creatures .... They had one the face of a man, and one the face of a lion, and one the face of a bull, and one the face of an eagle ..." (Ez. 1,10). Saint John the Evangelist describes the same forms in his Revelation: "In the centre (of heaven where stands the throne of God) were four animals with many eyes. ... The first animal was like a lion, the second like a bull, the third animal had a human face, and the fourth animal was like a flying eagle ..." (Rev. 4,6).

Saint Augustine and St. Jerome share the same opinion that the Lion symbolizes Mark because his Gospel starts in the desert with a voice crying "Prepare the way for the Lord ..." (Mark 1,3). The Bull symbolizes Luke because at the beginning of his Gospel he tells the story of Zachariah, the priest, who offered a bull as a sacrifice to the Lord (Luke 1,8). The human face symbolizes Matthew because he starts his Gospel by describing the human genealogy of our Lord (Matt. 1,1). Finally, the eagle symbolizes John because he opens his Gospel with the divine geneology of our Lord (John 1,1).

The icons of the Evangelists are generally full of brilliance and harmony. When the four are shown together in one panel it expresses the Christian belief that they all record the same pulse and write about the same person. They are in harmony, and proclaim the same truth of God. Their faces and attitudes shine with such warmth that one cannot help be fascinated by the message they have to offer. The tender tone in their coloring brings out their psychological attitude of peaceful humility and intense attentiveness. They touch us to the quick and make us, in turn, "attentive to their proclamation." Each has the features of a wise man, conscious of his purpose, of his immense responsibility, completely faithful to his inspiration.

When they have the Gospel in their hands, they do not hold it. They seem to be barely touching it out of immense respect and love. Their attitude is of those who know they have been privileged to propagate, in universal words, the mystery of the appearance of God, which they have been allowed to witness and record. The aura of their divine election is shown in the deep gold tone of the background.

Icons of the Lord, and of the events of his life as reported in the Gospels, are generally fixed in their form. They are almost unchangeable because they are inspired by the Word of God, and because they proceed from the unchangeable Spirit of God. The icon comes from the Word and is the visual perfection of the Word.

The canons or rules of iconography usually depict St. Matthew as a mature and impressive person, with grey hair and a full beard, imposing in every detail of his personality. St. Mark is usually depicted as a younger man, characterized by a certain human tenderness.

St. Luke is also shown as a younger man, strong with an attitude of firm determination. Some icons show him seated, completely plunged in a deep meditation or vision of the Lord. Other icons depict him intensely absorbed in painting an icon of the Mother of God. He is traditionally considered to be the first iconographer and to have established the rules of Christian iconography.

St. John is often pictured as an old man, dictating his Gospel to his secretary Prochoros. His inspiration is shown as coming from heaven. He looks intently to his right with his eyes fixed on a ray of light coming from God. Other popular icons show the inspiration from heaven as coming from an angel who whispers in his ear the words of the gospel.

Thus there is a special fascination in the icons of the Evangelists, and in the icons of every story and event related in the Gospels. One must use the inner eye, for which the outer eye is only an instrument, to understand and really enjoy the divine reality of the Gospel, the doorway to heaven and the key to the Kingdom.

8. - The Royal Road: Asceticism

The first application of the Greek word *theosis* or "divinization" was given to the Logos Incarnate, to Christ, because his human nature was infused with divine qualities and perfections. Theosis was also applied to human persons who, because of the Incarnation, were united with Christ and became divine in Christ. Finally, the word was used to describe the Body of Christ, the Church, which is Christ himself present in his Eucharistic Body and Blood, the "temple of God which is not made by human hands but by the Spirit of the Lord" (Heb. 9, 11).

This divinization, or theosis, this union of humanity with Christ, does not confuse the Creator and the created. The Creator is divinity and possesses all perfections in himself. He is above change and beyond becoming. We, on the other hand, are creatures who depend on God for existence, development, and growth and who have been made divine. We have to acquire perfections and grow in them through hard exercises and enormous efforts. Saint Macarios of Egypt says, "The One is God, the other is not; the One is Lord, and the other is servant; the One is Creator, and the other is creature." According to the Fathers theosis and the development of any bodily, spiritual, or intellectual perfection is acquired through reception of the sacraments reinforced by asceticism. Theosis and perfection are both gifts bestowed by God that must be developed and maintained by exercise.

Humans live in time. They cannot grow into any perfection, into discipleship to the Lord, or into the spirit of the Gospel without submitting themselves to time and to continual efforts of body and soul. God is Eternity, and he is essentially perfect in every perfection. A human being's growth into the perfection of God - "Be ye all perfect as Your heavenly Father is perfect" (Matt 5, 48) - is a long process, the struggle of a lifetime. This growth in perfection has no limit because it is a process leading to participation in the perfection of God. To become flames of the Spirit, possessors of any kind of perfection, we must exercise our whole lives. To attain to any perfection, we must continually be attentive to inspiration. The first step is to submit to discipline.

DISCIPLINE

In Christian language the three basic ideas behind the Greek word *asketicos* are well-balanced movement, intelligent control, and effective mastery. To become an ascetic one's entire faculties must be organized and directed toward simplicity so that the person's mind and body and spirit are free of unnecessary trappings that can weigh them down.

In order to achieve their unique perfections, ascetics must first liberate themselves from the egotistic interests and limited ambitions of nature. Asceticism, therefore, is noble and full of dignity, in spite of its seeming austere and unbending character. People who seek a better realization of their bodily, spiritual, or intellectual development must follow a rigid discipline and accept innumerable restraints self-imposed in order to battle in themselves the interior idolatry of temporary wants and personal interests that fetter and enslave.

Athletes train their bodies for outstanding achievements; artists seek the technical expertise they need to give form to their visions; scholars, scientists, and students seek patiently the clear light of knowledge; couples work together to create between themselves and with their families a mirror of the Divine Community; and many others hunger, thirst, lust, even burn and shiver with a longing that only God can satisfy.

Discipline is an inner drive of the will, a sap of life that runs through the fissures of our bodies and souls. It overcomes materiality and laziness, and infuses us with freedom, vitality, and grace. Discipline is born out of an inner flame, out of a vision that consumes us to such an extent that it directs all our faculties toward making us creators, saints, artists, people truly alive.

Only through the discipline of tremendous amounts of effort and renunciation can people really achieve inner freedom, and permit the likeness of God within them to emerge and reign. Any spiritual, physical, or intellectual perfection is, indeed, a beam of the light of God and of his radiance, a manifestation of what he is in his own Being. Any perfection is a radiance of God himself; when acquired, it makes us saints, holy, special people of God.

Discipline does not create love. Discipline does not create, in the musician, the love for music, or in the artist the dedication to art, or in the Christian the love for solitude and dedication to others. One must first be in love with God, with music, with dancing, with art, with science, with others, to have the courage to practice asceticism, and to go through the continual ordeals of the studio, of the novitiate, of self-control, of fast and abstinence, of study and exercise.

Discipline, be it connected with the studio for art, the laboratory for science, the home for family, or the novitiate for religious life, sustains and increases love and the fascination for perfection, but it does not create them. It makes the already existing love and fascination faithful, patient, and more enduring.

Discipline makes permanent also the hope that is in us. Hope is not listless waiting. It is the prolongation of an activity which is central to us, already rooted in our very beings. Hope is not mere wishful desire; hope is a will that strives toward higher realizations, refusing to calculate difficulties.

Hope is perfect relaxation in the powerful act of drawing out of one's self a hidden quality or a special perfection. It is an inner flame that keeps one alive and engenders the courage to accept difficulties in order to turn them into divine forms of the spirit. Indeed, to experience goodness and perfection and to achieve beauty, human beings have to be alert and alive. It is only the most intense saints, scientists, and artists who experience the exalted reaches of hope.

Hope and discipline and love keep us alert. They drive the saint into solitude for the encounter with God, the musician into the studio for the perfection of art, the ballet dancer or athlete to hard hours of exercise, and the husband and wife to face each other and their daily chores.

Difficulties and privations are irksome. But discipline, hope and love can make them a joy. For this reason ancient abbots did not allow their monks to fast until they first were aflame with love for others and for God. The underlying idea was that in order to become a harp that can vibrate to the touch of the Holy Spirit, a man or woman must first be in love. Once possessed by the radiance of God, the monk or the artist, the lovers or the scientist, can submit to the rigid regularity, discipline, direction, silence, and solitude, which in turn will increase and sustain their love. The saying that enfleshed this rule was that the "mystical life preceeds asceticism." No one can live a deep life, be it artistic, athletic, scientific, or spiritual, without first submitting to rigid discipline, sustained by hope and aflame with love. Long periods of meditation and physical exercises are only ways to sustain and uphold love and hope; they do not create them.

LADDER OF ASCENT

Since the second century, Christianity has been repeating, with Saint Irenaeus of Lyons, that the "glory of God is a man [or woman] fully alive." To be fully alive is to hope and to be in love. To hope deeply and to be deeply in love, one must first be healed of inner disorders. One must be free to be in love. Only in freedom can we hope to realize free to be in love. Only in freedom can we hope to realize our uniqueness as persons and allow God to manifest himself in us.

The first condition, the first step towards the act of hope and the art of loving, is to be free of one's self and of one's blind personal point of view. Only great watchfulness of body and spirit can bring about this freedom. A saint, an athlete, a scientist, a husband and wife who are one all are people who have freed themselves and risen to the level of their human uniqueness as persons. They are in permanent watchfulness for the revelation of their beloved, always ready to vibrate to an inspiration and to surrender to a call.

FREEING THE SELF

Ultimately, being fully alive and vibrant is being a sharer in the life of the Trinity, bathed in the goodness of God. "Only God is good," said the Lord (Matt. 19, 12). He is, indeed, all goodness, but we can participate in his goodness and live out what he is by allowing his image and likeness to shine forth in us.

People cannot reach the fullness of their human capacities, be alert and fully alive, except through an incessant fight against the false ego. "He who wants to follow me," said the Lord Jesus, "let him deny himself and take up his cross every day and follow me" (Matt. 16, 24). In order to be a hockey player, a scientist, a saint, a husband or wife, an artist, an entertainer, one must first be in love, and then be able to embrace daily painful experiences and difficult tasks. All human seekers of perfection, joy, and happiness must forget themselves and carry their daily crosses in order to find their uniqueness as persons.

Whoever we are, we cannot avoid responsibility and integrity if we are seeking any perfection. Each day we must take our lives into our own hands and put our distinct and unique stamp on them. We must freely create each day and give it a shape and a purpose rather than let circumstances rule our lives. This is what the Lord means by the command to deny the self and "carry the cross." To carry the cross every day on the road of life is to transform the raw material of life and make it beautiful. To reach our uniqueness as persons, we must die to ourselves, which is to crush our blind tendency to grab for immediate gratification; and we must learn to control our enslaving egos. We have to sell every security and every possession "to buy the pearl of inestimible value," (Matt. 13, 46).

Dying to one's self is not self-destruction or dissolution: it is a rising beyond the self. The Fathers called it *epectasis*, the going out of one's lesser self to rise to a higher reality of the self. Early rising, care of the body, punctuality, fasting, abstinence, faithfulness to studio exercises and home chores, peaceful and living acceptance of others: these are the many daily and hourly crosses one has to bear to realize one's own uniqueness as a person.

The Lord said again: "What would it profit a man to gain the whole world and lose his soul? Or what shall a man give in exchange for his soul?" (Matt. 16, 26) "Losing one's soul" is losing one's personality, the uniqueness, the freedom of the image of God in one's self, and falling into self-idolatry and self-hypnotism.

The cocoon has to be broken open; the caterpillar has to abandon a precious part of itself. It must die to itself first in order to find its uniqueness as a radiant butterfly. We have to maintain ourselves in a state of continual effort in order to vibrate to the touch of others. We have to come out of our selfish little egos, however dear, however precious they may be, to burst into the fullness of beauty.

The prophets could not have been prophets and proclaimed the message of God if they had not abandoned their own private little securities and found their inner freedom and uniqueness. At first they all resisted the call of God because of their own selfish, self-centered insecurities. But when they overcame these fears and vanities, they became the prophets the world remembers.

FULLNESS OF PERSONALITY

When the enslaving ego is vanquished and the conflicting inner desires are harmonized, God is mirrored in the soul, and we become our real selves, free and refreshed. Once peace engulfs our senses, and the light of God moves into the recesses of our being, our uniqueness is released, and we can stand alone and defy all the forces which seek to submerge us.

Then hermits find their fullness in solitude and perfect harmony in their relations with others; sinners, dancers, artists of all kinds achieve the pinnacles of creativity; wife and husband face each other and perform their daily chores with joy and enthusiasm. The inner life is a maze, and human beings cannot find the way to uniqueness unless this maze of human faculties is illuminated with the peace and harmony that asceticism can produce.

All saints, writers, athletes, artists, lovers, and scientists are fired with the same flame and the same vision. The flame is God, and the vision is the radiance of the face of God. All who practice their asceticism faithfully and joyfully are places where God lives and radiates the beauty of his reality in relationships, sounds, knowledge, and movements. God is the origin of the inspiration, its true object and final purpose.

Scientists are in the presence of God because they are touched by the truth of God; artists and athletes are in the presence of God because they are enraptured by the beauty of God in form, sound, colour, or motion; and saints are in the presence of God because they allow themselves to be caught up by the love of God so fully that they achieve perfect relationships with the person of God himself and with other human persons.

It is always God who is the origin and the center of all perfection. Even when the artist, the lover, the poet, the scientist, and the athlete cannot name him, God is the real reality behind their quest for perfection. Saints, scientists, actors, performers - all are stamped with a halo of glory and honor because God inhabits them with a special intensity.

St. Gregory of Nyssa teaches that holiness is nothing else but the unquenchable thirst, the intensity of the desire for God, sought in the perfection of our human endeavors. That is why the human soul cannot find repose except in the infinite reality of God. The saints are the essence of this desire.

The Church recognizes its saints by canonization. "Canon" means a list. The saints are put on the list of benefactors of humanity because they have left behind them a trail of light and goodness that leads to God as revealed by Christ. Sciences, academies, and organizations of artists also "canonize" their peers. They put their names on lists as the great benefactors of humanity. Thus we have Pulitzer Prizes, Emmy and Oscar Awards, Nobel Prizes, Halls of Fame, and many other forms of "canonization."

If God is real, he must be the captivating, compelling object of all humanity's attention, the center of attraction of all yearnings and realizations. Christians understand that God is present in all the great endeavors and realiations of humanity because God is real and is the enthralling center of humanity's longings. Christ calls them blessed. Christians see the majesty that rests upon all scientists, artists, lovers, and saints, and claims them as members of the same family of God, expressing God in the variety of his Wisdom.

If we allow our vision to be transformed by the Gospel, our eyes become so focused, and our hearts so attuned, that we recognize God in every way he chooses to reveal himself to his creation - in the arts, in the sciences, in the joy of living, as well as in the contemplation of his face. The joy of seeing God thus expressed in the variety of human endeavors amazes our hearts and stirs us to sigh in admiration of his goodness.

When the ballet dancer defies the laws of materiality and gravity, when the singer or entertainer can stand alone and bring joy to many, when a husband and wife can find paradise in each other, and when religious men and women bathe their bodies and souls in perfect peace and harmony, we all experience God and burst out in glorification of his goodness. This is why the Lord said in the Gospel, "Let your light shine before men, that they may see your good works and glorify your Father who is in heaven" (Matt. 5, 16).

This is the Christian vision and understanding of asceticism as inspired by the Incarnation and the presence of God in our flesh. Beside this Christian conception of asceticism there is also philosophical "moral asceticism."

9. - Moral Asceticism

In the sixth and fifth centuries before Christ, Zeno, the Greek philosopher, was the first theorist of moral asceticism, later called Cynicism. The famous Diogenes popularized Cynicism, which later came to be called Sophism, or "Wisdom." These philosophers built, with great intellectual acumen, the general theory that the human person was made to achieve inner freedom of the soul.

For Greek philosophers this inner freedom was the supreme virtue and sole aim of human life. Inner freedom is indifference to all social and personal satisfaction; it renounces all pleasures. Indifference and renunciation make the soul independent of the changing circumstances of the outer world. Thus, all sensual, intellectual, or scientific pleasures were considered slavery, darkness, and degradation. Consequently, all pleasures - learning, food and drink, riches and comfort, and above all any pleasure to be derived from the company of women - were to be avoided. Philosophical and social theorists practiced this moral asceticism and made it the center of their teaching.

In the second century after Christ, the Gnostics summarized all the teachings of moral asceticism in what they called the three seals: "the seal of the mouth," against food and drink; "the seal of the body," against any conforts; and "the seal of the womb," against any relationship with women.

The disgust felt for women owed its origin to oriental modes of thought and the belief that the body was evil; therefore anything that produced bodies (that is, women) were doubly evil. Greek philosophy and Cynic teaching popularized these ideas, and Greek and Roman cultures adopted this teaching and put it into rigorous practice.

In the first century before Christ and long after, thousands of Cynic and stoic preachers were seen in every part of the Roman empire and heard in every corner of every city. They were so powerful that they deeply influenced many religious communities in both Jewish and pagan circles. The Jewish sect of Essenes followed them and practiced the strictest moral rules, showing great zeal and heroism. They lived in isolation and in bitter opposition to the world which they considered to be evil.

Such an attitude became very popular in the second and third centuries. Consciences were aroused. The most vivid and graphic language, frequently pungent and sweeping, was used to attack the shallowness of ordinary living. The movement gained so much momentum and importance that it infiltrated all Roman and Greek society, and even Church teaching.

ASCETICISM IN THE EARLY CHURCH

At the time of the Apostles, and during the first century, one very familiar sight in the Roman empire was pagan and Jewish Cynics, wearing rough cloaks, carrying begging bags and thorn sticks. They wandered from town to town, preaching to the people and hammering in their moral platitudes. Zeal and enthusiasm for this type of "moral virtue" fired up Christians also.

When the Apostles went preaching the Gospel, they traveled about in a similarly unencumbered manner. Christians everywhere thought that their missionaries were no less important than Greek philosophers, and no less worthy of attention. Thus, it came about that people living at that time confused the Christian ideal of denying the world for the sake of the Kingdom of God with the Cynic idea of despising the world for the sake of personal isolation; they thus overlooked the lesson of the Incarnation which is to create the most harmonious relation between mind and matter.

The Apostles and early Christian accepted, for instance, continence as a sacred way of life, and they even enforced it because they were expecting the *Parousia*, the end of the world and the final coming of Christ at any moment. The teaching of St. Paul was clear and urgent that the end of the world and the coming of Christ were imminent. It was not much use, Paul believed, to get entangled with a wife, a husband, or children. He felt the worries of this world would hinder people from preparing to receive the Lord. "The time is short," he said, "... those who have wives be as though they have not... for the fashion of this world passes away ..." (1 Cor. 7, 29-31).

The general cultural climate of Christians, especially in areas around the Mediterranean, was deeply steeped in pagan practices. In this Greco-Roman area which was also influenced by Eastern thought, laws of purity for pagan priests were very prominent. Rules of "ritual purity" were common, very respected, and obeyed: "Anyone who approaches the altar must not have enjoyed the pleasures of Venus the night before." This rule was adopted by the Church in an even stricter way because the Christian altar was loftier and more sacred than the pagan.

This liturgical law of abstinence was given even more importance because of the Stoic ideal of "equanimity." Sexual intercourse was called a "little epilepsy." It robs people of their senses and therefore is not "in accord with reason." Christians were products of their age. They were deeply influenced and deeply penetrated by the culture of their time. "Omnis coitus immundus" says Saint Jerome: "Any sexual intercourse is impure."

This rule of "ritual purity" was accepted by both Churches, Eastern and Western alike. After a variety of vain attempts to make purity a general ideal for all Christians, the Church of Rome officially promulgated, at the Second Lateran Council in 1139, the law of celibacy, binding only the clergy and those seeking ordination. (See *Mystique et Continence*, Etudes Carmelitaines, Paris-Bruges, 1952 pp. 51-60).

ASCETICISM IN THE GOSPEL

The Gospel of our Lord Jesus Christ offers a striking contrast to this teaching of Greek philosophers and to this oriental mentality. The contrast is clearly seen if one compares the attitude of our Lord to that of John the Baptist, who represents the Old Testament and the best of the pagan teaching of his time. John the Baptist was an ascetic according to the Greek philosophical teaching and Jewish tradition. Our Lord was not. John the Baptist lived in the solitude of the desert away from crowds and populated centers. He wore a tunic woven of camel hair and a belt made of leather. His food was grasshoppers and the honey of wild bees. He and his disciples made frequent fasts; they shunned marriage and the company of women.

Our Lord Jesus Christ had no rule about the frequentation of women, or about food and drink, and he imposed none on his apostles. He never shunned the company of women, who are seen throughout the Gospels surrounding him. The Gospels gratefully remember the names of some of these women: Mary Magdalen, Joanna, Suzanna, and several others. These women and "many others," says Luke, were with him, and they provided out of their own resources for all his needs and the needs of his disciples. They not only placed their means at the disposal of the Lord, they even wove for him the cloaks which he wore to the end of his life.

Our Lord sought solitude only on occasion. But most of the time he worked in big cities and towns, at the lakeside, and always in the presence of great crowds. He ate and drank with tax-collectors and sinners, and he accepted the invitations of well-to-do Pharisees. He never shunned the company of sinners.

Our Lord exemplified the perfection of a person who does not need, and consequently does not practice, asceticism. As God, he "played" in his own personal experience healing the sick, raising the dead, wiping the tears of mankind, and changing the water of our humanity into the heady wine of divinity. Christ could do all this because he was totally free. He was a flame of perfection that none of our human failures could ever hinder. Christ did not need to practice moral asceticism.

The contrast between the Lord, the perfectly free man, and John, the ascetic, is striking, but it reveals merely a difference in a way of life, not in essential attitude. Our Lord clearly expressed the view that to be his disciple, to live his way of life and enter the Kingdom, it is necessary to break all the bonds that enslave us. If anything offers a hindrance and opposes the flow of God's life into our hearts, then our seductive love must be met with a blow: "No man can serve two masters; for either he will hate the one and love the other; or else he will hold to the one and despise the other. You cannot serve God and Mammon" (Matt. 6, 24; Luke 16, 13).

Scientists who betray the honest, humble quest for truth for prestige or position; artists who betray their art for fashion or adulation; athletes who betray their bodies for a temporary victory; lovers who betray their beloved for egotism; saints who betray holiness for self-admiration or notoriety - all have chosen Mammon over God.

Furthermore, for the Lord, anything that distracts from God, anything that enslaves us, that leads our hearts away from perfect love, must be repudiated. He called us to freedom and perfect love. To be his disciples is to be free and to love. His Word demands that we be strong, valiant, and powerful. He commands us to "hate," which is to reject anyone or anything that would enslave us, make us less than we can be, or prevent us from achieving the freedom of being his disciples. "If any man come to me, and does not hate his mother and father and wife and children, and brothers and sisters, indeed, and his own life also, he cannot be my disciple" (Luke 14, 26).

MONACHISM

Monachism means living alone by one's self. Monachism was created by this desire for a freedom born of love. Christian monachism was inaugerated not by philosophers or clerics but by the *fellaheen*, the peasant-farmers of Christian Egypt, who first sought solitude in the corner of a garden or in a back room of their homes.

Monachism, or the practice of solitude, did not originally include separation from family, home, or social surroundings. It was only when the idea of seeking moral perfection by fleeing the world and shunning society was considered possible that some Christians generously gave up both society and the world. But this did not become a general practice until the third century.

In the year 250, when Decius, the Roman Emperor, waged a persecution against the Christians, he exiled them to the desert, to mountains and to remote areas. The exiled ones, filled already with grace and love, discovered that the dreaded curse of exile was really a special blessing. They found solace and peace in their solitude, extolled its benefits, and came to consider it a necessity. They found a special comfort because they could practice their religious worship without outside interference. They remained in the deserts and mountains and thus became the first hermits.

Saint Anthony popularized the practice, and Saint Athanasius, who wrote Anthony's life, made monachism known all over the world. Monastic spirituality - this perennial spring of spiritual life - was first lived and written about in the East. The modern Dominican and Jesuit, the nun and the monk, the teaching brother and the secular priest of today, are still quenching their thirst in the divine Nile of the Egyptian desert.

While one of the influences of monachism may have been the flight from persecution, it seems also that another positive influence was much stronger. When, in the fourth century, Constantine the Great brought freedom to Christianity, suddenly untold numbers of converts from paganism flocked to the Church. Christians suddenly found themselves occupying the coziest and most luxurious places in Roman civilization. For the first time in the history of Christianity, it was easy to be a Christian. Lukewarmness infiltrated hearts and souls and led to a gradual cooling and eventual freezing of idealism. Morals relaxed. Pagan practices also infiltrated the Church and found there a new home and new practitioners. This avalanche of worldliness provoked a violent reaction in the fervent who then fled to the solitude of the desert away from the corruption.

For the first three centuries, before political and social freedom came to the Church, when Christians were persecuted, they always aspired to "martyrdom" for the sake of Christ. Now that they had become free and accepted in the empire, aspirations for martyrdom were replaced in the hearts of many by the moral rigors of the Stoics, Sophists, and Manicheans of their time. They practiced moral virtue with more zeal than any of their pagan predecessors. In the fourth century, monachism developed into a great movement that captured the fancy of the educated and the ignorant alike.

Christians fled to the solitudes of the deserts and mountains by the thousands. Their leaders and organizers are called "desert fathers." These hermits lived in the deserts of Egypt in the same peace and simplicity as their forerunners.

In the fourth century there were two main practices in vogue among them. Some lived as hermits off on their own. Others lived in a sort of community, a loosely knit body of men under the rule of a "shepherd," or *Abba*, a "father," but following their own individual bent as far as penance and occupations went. These communities (cenobitic monasticism) often numbered in the thousands. Some lived exemplary lives of holiness, detachment, and love for others; and some left their doors wide open to abuses, laxity, rivalries, and sometimes over-severity on the part of too zealous leaders.

Under the strong influence of Manichean preaching, matter and the human body came to be considered evil by many hermits. This led them to eccentricity; they even tried to kill the senses and all human sensitivity. Bizarre penances, street preachers, and fanatical pilgrims, stirred much excitement all over the empire with their unusual practices. They tortured their bodies by untold privations and cruelties. And when they discovered that the passions created by God were more resistant than they expected, they doubled their cruelties. Fortunately, this absurd way of life did not endure long.

SAINT BASIL

Reform and organization needed a well-balanced person, steeped in the Gospel and in human understanding. Basil of Caesaria in Asia Minor was well trained in Greek learning and in the solid common sense of the East. Both these qualities were perfectly united in his sister Macrina, who was the originator of the idea that "a community of devoted Christians, living in continence and under the strictest discipline, served God better than the wild-eyed anchorites" (Robert Payne, *The Holy Fire*, p. 116). Her community of women were the first monks in the true sense of the word. Fired by her example, Basil made a trip through Egypt, Palestine, Syria, and Mesopotamia, visiting the *athletae Dei*, the athletes of God; then he came home to establish a community of men like the community of women that Macrina had already founded.

Basil's main idea was that every monastery should be not only an assembly in which each would labor for the benefit of all but also a community in which all submitted to the obedience of a "shepherd," who was to be guided by a definite rule. For the first time in history, the three fundamental virtues of monachism - poverty, chastity, and obedience - were explicitly formulated by Saint Basil; later they were adopted everywhere in Christianity.

St. Basil directed his monks toward the communal life and wrote his special rule which became in both the East and the West the classical model for all subsequent rules of monastic life. He also definitely directed the monastic mentality away from the hermitical or eremitical ideal toward life in common. Organized monasticism was established. Monks lived together under one rule in permanent contact with each other and with the world. Monasticism was born.

MONASTICISM

Monasticism means to be alone, but in a community of brothers or sisters who live together under the leadership of a spiritual father or mother.

At first, under the influence of Greek Cynicism and Sophism, both hermits and monks scorned learning, philosophy, and all intellectual activity. They considered them to be too worldly and too remote from the truth of Christ and the Gospels. But, "When the 'mind' ceased to be opposed to matter, because Christian monasticism fully accepted the implications of the Incarnation," (John Myendorff, *Gregory Palamas*, p. 3) monks accepted also scientific knowledge and became themselves champions of all learning. They saved Greek and Roman cultures from oblivion and decay. Fourth century monasticism produced great philosophers and theologians and the great Fathers of the Church.

ST. BENEDICT

At that time, and up to the end of the fifth century, some monasticism existed in the West, but it was considered for a long time an Eastern import. St. Benedict (480-547) organized western monasticism on the model of St. Basil's spirit and rule. With Saint Benedict the monastery became a "school for divine worship" entirely devoted to the coming of the Kingdom. Monks submitted to "definite stability" and owed obedience to an *Abba* or Abbot whom they elected for life.

Relations among monks and with the outside world were carefully determined and organized hierarchically. Prayer (ora), work (labora) and meditation on the word of God (lectio divina) divided equally the days of their lives. In the Western church monks became progressively more influential in the administration of their Church and eventually acquired unlimited civil power as well. Because they had a monopoly on learning for a time, they became the sole defenders of the city and civilization against barbarian invasions. For a long time also they were the only ones who wrote laws for both Church and state. The whole Western world was submitted to the influence of the Church for centuries to come because of the monks.

The formation and guidance of Christian consciences was also in their hands. For centuries any moral or intellectual excellence was to be obtained only in monasteries and convents. In prayer and contemplation, great minds, artistic abilities, and new scientific methods were developed. They invented systems of thought in the sciences and in the arts. Their methods became the foundations for all our modern sciences, philosophies, social studies, technologies, and all learning.

SPIRITUAL VALUE OF MONASTICISM

People who enter Christian monasteries do not retire from the world because they hate or despise the world, but because they love the world and care for its welfare. By retiring from the world, they seek to protect the world from its own hysteria and self-neglect. Genuine solitude seeks to recreate man and to perfect humanity, not to destroy it. It is the search for genuine communion with the world, material and human, and definitely not a self-seeking enterprise.

Christians become monks because a fire burns in them with such intensity that they can no longer tolerate a mediocre life confined to the valleys. Their asceticism is born from, and sustained by, this flame. "They are irresistably drawn toward the pure and calm stillness of the snow-capped mountain tops, where one forgets to look at the earth, but stretches one's hands toward the stars."

Men and women become monks and nuns to turn their eyes away from the present time, the present earth, the present condition of human nature, to hang their wedding garment and their loneliness in the closet of eternity. They have no fear or hesitation to choose solitude instead of family life in the world because they know that they will recover their humanity in all its beauty and glory in the company of other brothers or sisters. They know also that they will rise again out of the grave, transformed with a special glory, illumined, strengthened, and penetrated by divinity. Their special asceticism is a most precious gift which inspires them and keeps their resolve strong and joyous.

In spite of occasional deviations, exaggerations, and shortcomings, our Christian monasteries have been and still are, in both East and West, places aglow with pure, unselfish love, dedication, and goodness. The asceticism of poverty, chastity, and obedience are spiritual commitments of body and soul, mind and heart, consistent with the ideals of the Gospel. This is asceticism in one of its most glorious expressions. Monks "try on truths for size" and discover that these truths can serve humanity for all occasions, provided one wears them with humility, discrimination, and dedication, led by prayer and the Holy Spirit.

ASCETICISM IN MARRIAGE

Less spoken of or written about, but chosen by more people, is the asceticism of Christian marriage. A Christian marriage takes place when two people stand face to face and say to each other: "I would rather find my way into God's love with you than by myself. Come with me. Take my hand, and let us combine our strength and our vision and help each other to our God."

Like monks, the Christian couple must give up all self-centeredness. They must decide what is enough materially for themselves and for their families while living in a society that glorifies the acquision of material possessions. They must practice the chastity of marriage, which is not abstinence from sexual love, but the controlling and channelling of that love for the good and benefit of each other, and for the cooperation with God and the universe in the creation of life. And they must learn obedience, each to the wishes and desires of the other as they grow together into one flesh.

FASTING: ASCETICISM IN THE LITURGY

The asceticism of fast and abstinence is not a Christian invention or monopoly. It has always been common to humanity as a means for better physical health and as an aid for improving intellectual activity and contemplative endeavors. We Christians use fasting and abstinence as an affirmation of freedom in regard to one's own ego and self-centeredness. The voluntary interruption of the rhythm of our basic desires and pleasures in food, human physical relations, and superficial intellectual curiosity is, indeed, a means to deeper inner tranquility and clearer contemplation. This ritualizing of life does not lead into narrowness and rigidity but to an existential experience.

For the monk, poverty, chastity, and obedience are the way of the weak in the presence of the mighty instinct. Fasting and voluntary hunger, like chastity and obedience, are as positive and as spiritual as they are corporal. It is the mastery of a fundamental instinct, a struggle of restraint and self-limitation. Hunger, chastity, and obedience, imposed on people by others, sour into bitterness and despair. Hunger, chastity, and obedience, chosen and accepted freely, melt into self-knowledge, awareness of personal needs, limitations, possibilities, and potential. They also help identify one's self with the sufferings of the ill-fed and the ill-loved.

Fast and abstinence bring us closer to the brother and the sister who are hungry and in need of human tenderness. Christians know that they are members of the one family of God, called to uphold each other and build up the family which is on pilgrimage to Paradise.

In a special way, fasting and abstinence are for the Christian as necessary a preparation for a significant celebration as they are for artists and professionals who prepare for a special performance. Feeding on silence, calm and peace, makes one alive to God, and makes God a part of one's own flesh. In silence and chastity, in obedience and calm, we cease to be devoured by haste and action, and it becomes easy for our faculties to vibrate to the touch of the Holy Spirit. We become non-poisonous, ready to understand and accept our neighbors, and to be understood and accepted by them.

Saint John Chrysostom sums up the meaning of Christian fasting in these words:

"Fasting is a medicine. But like all medicines, though it be very profitable to the person who knows how to use it, it frequently becomes useless and even harmful in the hands of him who is unskillful in its use.

"I have said these things, not that we may disparage fasting, but that we may honor fasting. For the honor of fasting consists not in abstinence from food, but in withdrawing from sinful practices, since he who limits his fasting only to abstinence from meats is one who especially disparages fasting.

"So you fast? Give me proof of it by your works. These are the type of works: If you see a poor man, take pity on him. If you see an enemy, be reconciled with him. If you see a friend gaining honor, do not be jealous of him... Let the hands fast by being pure from plundering and avarice... Let the feet fast... Let

the eyes fast... (Looking is the food of the eyes.) Let the ears also fast by refusing to receive evil or idle talks and calumnies... Let the mouth fast from disgraceful speeches and railings...

"For what does it profit if we abstain from fish and fowl and yet bite and devour the brother and sister. The speaker of evil eats the flesh of his brother and sister, and bites the body of his neighbor. You have not fixed your teeth in his flesh but you have fixed your slander in his soul and inflicted the wound of evil suspicion, and you have harmed in a thousand ways yourself and him, and many others; for in slandering your neighbor you have made him who listens to the slander worse, for should he be a wicked person, he becomes more careless, when he finds a partner in his wickedness. And should he be a just person, he is tempted to arrogance and gets puffed up, being led on by the sin of others to imagining great things concerning himself. Beside this you have struck at the common welfare of the Church herself, for all those who hear you will not only accuse the supposed sinner, but the entire Christian community (John Chrysostom, *Concerning the Statues, Homily 3*).

PERIODS OF FAST

Fasts and abstinences are carefully distributed throughout the course of the liturgical calendar according to the seasons of the year. The two most important periods of fasting are in late fall and early spring.

At the end of winter and early spring we have the forty days of Lent, which is a preparation for the life of Resurrection, hope, joy, and salvation of the universe. The second most important fast is the forty days' preparation for the appearance of God in the flesh: Christmas, the illumination of darkness, and healing from the gloom of night.

In the summer also there is a fifteen-day preparation for the great event of the Dormition of the Mother of God. As Christ our God penetrated the universe with his human, male body at the Incarnation and Ascension, so at her

Dormition the Mother of God penetrated the heavens in her female body.

The Dormition is a day of glory for humanity, and specifically for femininity and womanhood. Preparation for such a celebration by fasting and abstinence is most appropriate, even necessary.

CONCLUSION

Asceticism of body and soul brings peace and beauty to the artist in the studio, perseverance to the athlete in the field, patience and hope to the scientist in the laboratory, and ecstacy of love to the monk and nun in their solitude, to husband and wife in their union. Asceticism of body and soul sustains monks and nuns in self-effacement, as it enlightens scientists, inspires musicians, strengthens athletes, and guides Christian couples. It engenders an ever freshly renewed vision of beauty.

Ascetics stand in readiness always attentive to the voice of God and to the call of the other. Their motto is "My brother ... My sister is my life!" And their ultimate cry of triumph and plenitude of joy is summarized by Saint Paul in these words: "I live - no, not I. It is Christ who lives in me!" (Gal. 2,20)

Asceticism is the key to the Kingdom.

10. - The Kingdom

Since Christ our Lord was God of God, and possessed the fullness of being, he moved in his divinity freely, joyously, precisely because divinity was his personal experience. His whole teaching in the Gospel is his own life, a poem of God, expressing God's freedom and God's beauty. The central theme and leit-motif of this teaching is the "Kingdom of God."

The Kingdom of God, according to Our Lord and Savior Jesus Christ, is the eruption of divine life into this universe. It is God himself, Father-Son-Spirit, penetrating humanity and all the events of our life, shaping our destiny. It is divinization in action! Being in the Kingdom is being in the life of the Trinity and sharing the life of God. The prayer of holy Baptism keeps on repeating the same theme again and again: "We are no longer children of the body but children of the Kingdom."

HUMAN DIGNITY AND WORTH

In his teaching, and in all the actions of his life, the Lord insisted on the value of the human person who is, he said, of divine origin. He insisted on the fact that the human person came from the overflow of life and love of the Father, the *Abba*, and consequently, that our origin was divine. Our Lord never once talked about abstract concepts like "human dignity" or "human rights." But he celebrated human dignity and human rights in no uncertain terms whenever he encountered a human being. In fact, he recognized human dignity and human rights in the most unlikely situations, where great thinkers and philosophers would falter and err.

The Samaritan on the road to Jericho was, for Christ, a noble human being. The adulteress thrown at his feet should have been stoned to death and put to a shameful destruction according to the law of Moses. But the Lord looked at her and immediately dismissed her in peace without condition or hesitation. The Samaritan woman was an abomination even to the Samaritans because of the scandals of her life. But to the Lord she was a person whom he honored. He even invited himself into her company unconditionally, without attempting first, as a condition, to convert her to another way of life. Zacchaeus, the abhorred extortioner, was given the special honor and privilege of receiving our Lord at his table. All the actions of Christ in the Gospel celebrate human dignity spontaneously, joyously, without any consideration other than that the human person is sacred and a child of God.

We Christians know that God made us not because he hated us but because he loved us. He made the universe not out of hatred, but out of love. And he declared that what he had made "was good." So, humanity and creation came out of a divine love, out of the heart of *Abba*.

If our origin is divine, we know that our present state of being is also divine. In the Incarnation, God the Son identified himself with us in our human flesh; he shared in our humanity to make us share in his divinity. In his Resurrection, we all rose to divine life. When he ascended into heaven, he placed our human nature at the right hand of the Father. In the Creed we proclaim that, "He ascended into heaven and sits at the right hand of God the Father." Sitting at the right hand of the Father means occupying a place of honor and glory with God.

The Father made us, the Son saved us, and the Holy Spirit flooded us with the life of the divine presence. By coming down on earth in the form of a dove, the Spirit manifested peace and harmony with existing humanity. The Spirit

The Kingdom

also came down in the form of a flame which filled creation with the fire of divinity, a fire that "burns but does not consume," as we say in our liturgical prayer. This is our God: Trinity, Father-Son-Spirit, spilling over into this world. This is why Christians affirm that the Kingdom of God is the eruption of divine life into the world, the merging of the Eternal with our human reality, bringing it to fullness.

Because they are in the "Kingdom of God," creation and the human race are secure in God. The faith of the Christian is unshakable, and his optimism is all pervading, because he knows that "all will be well, and all will be well, and all manner of things will be well .... It may, sometimes, look all wrong; but all will be well because we are in the Kingdom" (Julian of Norwich). Our Lord Jesus Christ wanted our life on earth to be a life like his own, overflowing with freedom, renewal, and resurrection. He wanted our life to be a celebration, like his own, radiant like the "lilies of the fields," and free like "the birds of the sky." He wanted it to be beautiful, filled with light and joy.

THE VISION OF CHRIST

Christ taught that the Kingdom, which is in us, is from an *Abba*, who comes to us continually in an immense movement of incarnation, upholding the cosmos and directing history. It is the Spirit who is the breath of the human person, and it is Christ himself who is Resurrection, Celebration of life, baptismal Grace, Plenitude of eucharist, Glorification, and Light of the whole of existence.

When the Lord talks about the Kingdom, he does not employ human words or any system of philosophy. When he delivers his message on the Kingdom, he does not use abstract concepts. The Lord's announcement of the Kingdom is described with excitement. The Kingdom is a great divine miracle. There is no need, says the Lord, to look around for the Kingdom, or to lie in wait in case someone says! "It is here, it is there." "The coming of the Kingdom of God," he says, "does not admit of observation, and there will be no one to say, 'Look here! Look there!' For you must know that the Kingdom of God is among you" (Luke 17, 20).

The Lord does not even explain. He points to a reality, and he chooses to use the events of nature, already charged with powerful suggestions, to awaken our heart and enflame our imagination. Once he likened the Kingdom to a mustard seed. At other times he compared it to a banquet, and to a precious coin lost in a stack of hay. A seed looks ordinary, frail, and insignificant. But it is rich with power and potentialities.

The Lord told another parable. He said: "The Kingdom of God is like a treasure hidden in a field which someone has found. He hides it again, goes off happy, sells everything he owns, and buys the field ...." And again he said: "The Kingdom is like a merchant looking for fine pearls; when he finds one of great value he goes and sells everything he owns and buys it ..." (Matt. 13, 44). Even buried in the mud, a pearl is rich in beauty and retains the value of a pearl. After a little cleaning it will sparkle on royal crowns.

These stories of our Lord transpose the ineffable and the incommunicable into happy dreams. Our Lord stirs up blazing passion for insoluble riddles. Ardor, generosity, and openness to the new, without pessimism about the past, require moral excellence and continual asceticism. To be a saint, a lover, or to build a community, is to be in the Kingdom, is to be inhabited by the Spirit of God, is to be consumed with an inner flame of love.

Christ God never imposed an obligation on our freedom. He does not force our will to accept the Kingdom, or even to renounce anything for its sake. True, we must renounce some things if we want to enter the Kingdom. But Christ never infringes on our freedom and liberty. He does not impose rules and regulations. Our Lord simply suggests, invites, and entices our will. Once we have recognized its preciousness, the Kingdom becomes an object worth all the sacrifices of life. Once we have realized that we are its inheritors and the honored guests at its banquet, we will then spontaneously sell everything to possess it. The Lord only points out the road to follow so that we can journey towards the Kingdom. He said that the merchant "goes out and sells everything to possess it." The Lord only points out the road to follow so that we can journey towards the Kingdom. He said that the merchant who found the pearl of great value also went and "sold everything he owned" to buy it. The Lord taught us to express an ardent desire and a great longing for the Kingdom. He urges us to sigh, "Thy kingdom come!"

THE VISION OF THE CHRISTIAN

In order to give up everything, we must first understand that our dignity resides in being possessors of the Kingdom. To rise to this great and adventuresome challenge, we must "leave" ourselves, achieve an "*ex-tasis*" of communion, be ready to abandon all our apparent securities and be free of compulsion. The Kingdom is planted in our very hearts, and it is in our hearts that it will bloom into glory and salvation. Our heart hears the voice of God, not in sounds and words, but by entering into the intimacy of his Person.

A hush must precede hearing, and inner silence is the only place where God reveals himself. In listening, our energies are focused in a moment of concentration, and we capture the revelation of God. To pray is to enter into the intimacy of another and to admit the other into our own intimacy. It is to see and be seen, to reveal one's self and to receive , the revelation of another. Prayer is to receive the revelation of God. The Kingdom is indeed within us, surrounding us, and not merely knocking at the door. It is the yeast in the bowl of dough which will leaven the whole batch if we are patient and wait in silence for it to rise. The Kingdom is in the very fibers of our body and soul like the mustard seed in the bowels of the earth. Prayer will bring it out and make us ready to hear the revelation and respond to it.

Prayer is listening to the hidden life that will come to bloom and grow in its own time. "Even when we say words and discourses in prayer," says Origen, "it is only to be able to listen better to the voice of God," to empty ourselves from distractions and let ourselves be invaded. For God to take hold of us and fill us with life, we must first be transparent and available. "So I will allure her; I will lead her to the desert and speak to her heart" (Hos. 2, 16), are the words God offers his beloved. The heart is the most central point of the human person, the place where the Kingdom is planted.

HUMAN DIGNITY AND THE LAW

In the Kingdom, we can no longer put our confidence in moral laws and obligations to save us. Laws that impose moral codes fetter our natural growth and development.

In the Old Testament, and in many other religions and human systems of behaviour, righteousness is always evaluated according to rules and regulations. In the Gospel, righteousness is a grace. Justice is not a juridical act that dispenses punishment for evil and reward for good. It is, rather, love, shown in freeing the oppressed and delivering the enslaved. God is faithful to his promise of salvation. Justice really means, on the part of God, the help God bestows on the poor and on the needy.

According to Jesus Christ, any one may enter the Kingdom - the despised and the lost, the tax collectors and the sinners, the sick and the poor, anyone who wishes. In the Kingdom, there is more joy over one sinner who repents than over ninety-nine "righteous persons" who, on account of their very "righteousness," do not feel the urgency or the necessity to come closer to God. The story of the Pharisee and the Publican brings out this wonderful teaching of the Lord.

The popular belief of the people of the Old Testament was that God was a righteous Judge who dealt with men's deeds exactly in accordance with the written Code of the Torah. The Jews believed that their own good works would receive a just reward, and their sins a punishement.

But Christ's preaching about the Kingdom radically altered this view. Christ taught us that God was like the employer who at different times in the day engaged people to work in his vineyard. At the end of the day he gave them all the same wages, saying to those who complained about his indiscriminate dealing: "You who were engaged first have received what was agreed upon. Why are you envious because I have been generous to those engaged last?" In the Kingdom of Christ, all righteousness is simple divine grace.

John Chrysostom proclaims this teaching of Christ in a magnificently eloquent passage in his homily of Easter. Our Church has been chanting it with vibrant faith for more than fifteen hundred years, from Antioch to the Bosphoros, from Africa to China, from the farthest steppes of Russia to the plains of the Ukraine and central Europe:

Let all pious men and all lovers of God rejoice in the splendor of this feast; let the wise servants blissfully enter into the joy of their Lord; let those who have borne the burden of Lent now receive their pay, and those who have toiled since the first hour, let them now receive their due reward; let any who came after the third hour be grateful to join in the feast, and those who may have come after the sixth, let them not be afraid of being too late, for the Lord is gracious and He receives the last even as the first. He gives rest to him who comes on the eleventh hour as well as to him who has toiled since the first; yes, He has pity on the last and He serves the first; He rewards the one and is generous to the other; he repays the deed and praises the effort.

Come, all of you: enter into the joy of your Lord. You the first and you the last, receive alike your reward; you rich and you poor, dance together you sober and you weaklings, celebrate the day; you who have kept the fast and you who have not, rejoice today. The table is richly loaded; enjoy its royal banquet. The calf is a fatted one; let no one go away hungry. All of you enjoy the banquet of faith; all of you receive the riches of his goodness. Let no one grieve over his poverty, for the universal kingdom has been revealed; let no one weep over his sins, for pardon has shone from the grave; let no one fear death, for the death of our Savior has set us free; He has destroyed it by enduring it, He has despoiled Hades by going down into its kingdom, He has angered it by allowing it to taste of his flesh.

Compassion, justice, and holiness are essential elements of the Kingdom. Justice and compassion are not the observation of established rules, but the caring that approaches the ordinary and the extraordinary of human life with equal ease and joy. The teaching of our Lord is that the legal preciseness which was so important in Pharisaic circles would not be sufficient for those who belong to the Kingdom. God is not satisfied with the outer fulfillment of commands.

LIFE IN THE KINGDOM

In the Kingdom, it is the heart, and not the enslavement to rules, that matters. Rules and commandments do not enslave or bind the Christian; they are rather a luminous vision. They shine as the little candle of daily life, and change all its details into vitality and joy.

When our Lord came he accepted not only the poor and the suffering but also the sinners, because God is near to them and calls them to himself. When the "friends" who were invited to the wedding feast failed to respond to the invitation of the divine Host, he sent messengers into the streets and public lanes to bring in the beggars and the crippled, the lame and the blind (Luke 14, 23). Those who search their hearts and come to the Father, enter the

Kingdom. The seeds of the Kingdom are replete with divine power.

Life in the Kingdom, as preached by our Lord, is not simply a reality reserved for a future time. It is available now, to all those who seek and accept God's nearness. Many Christians do not enjoy the Kingdom as the fullness of reality because the modern mind seeks to anlayze it, program it, control it. We are so dependent on our own successes or failures that our experiences of the spiritual life become disgracefully limited and embarrassingly thin. We fail to see the Kingdom of God in the present moment. The sacraments and the feasts of the life of Christ call attention to the true depth and meaning of our present life, transformed in the present moment. The Kingdom is present. We must become aware of it and enjoy its goodness now. We must always be ready to seize it and rest in it now, as our moment of grace.

If we were delicately and distinctively attuned to the present reality of God, we would never enslave ourselves or others. Christians live in harmony with others because they are in harmony with themselves, and because they live in harmony with God in the now of the Kingdom. They are in touch with the whole cosmos. They affirm the intrinsic goodness of everything and of everyone because they are always in touch with him who is the source of everything and of everyone.

Christians who are in the Kingdom are open to love because they know that there is a relation of love between them and God, and that they are loved. They proclaim goodness because they experience goodness. With God, they see life like a river flooding the whole land and sweeping away every hindrance. There is nothing left uncovered by its waves.

They who dwell in the Kingdom are primarily members of a community. They who live in peace and love with others are mirrors of their God who is a perfect community, Father-Son-Spirit. We Christians grow into full persons when we, individually, realize our interdependence with others in the Body of Christ. We are separated from the world only in the sense of coming together to form the heart of the world. We have freely responded to the call of God and formed a special community called the Church. It is through the Church that God brings about the regeneration not only of people but the whole of creation as well. The Kingdom, for the Christian, is a prophetic reality.

SUMMARY OF ALL VISIONS

Some monks of a large community living in complete solitude were puffed up by the thought that, because of their constant recitation of the psalms, they were surpassing others in virtue. They received this admonition from their Spiritual Father: "Do not tell me how often you fast and abstain, how many times you repeat the prayer and sing the psalms. There is something greater. There is, for the real Christian, the command of the Gospel of Our Lord Jesus Christ to be concerned for others. Is there any among you who can understand the tired mankind of our day, any who can suffer with those who suffer? Is there any one who can free those who have fallen into the snares of sin? Is there anyone who can provide peace to men who are in need of peace? He who can enable them to come to love life and to rejoice and be thankful for life, and thus build up the community of God, this one is the real disciple of Christ."

People of the Kingdom throb with sympathy for every human person. If they see their brothers afflicted with any anxiety, they yearn after their welfare. They never feel a need to compare themselves with anyone else. They waste no energy in refuting hostile opinions. They do not convert; they lead others to religious experience. They do not moralize; they reveal the true dignity of those who are to inhabit the Kingdom. Their inspiration comes from above, from the inner working of their being in the Kingdom of God. They can only radiate peace and confidence. They are not crusaders, because their strength is chaste and limpid. Christians are not in heaven or in the Kingdom; the Kingdom and heaven are in Christians.

Those who are filled with the Kingdom will grow in their humanity and will radiate an inward dignity in everything they do; nothing in their lives will be casual or left to chance. Their every thought and deed will be robed in the splendid vestments of a divine and holy liturgy. The more conscious they are of their divine origin, of their present divine state and divine destiny, the more joy there will be in their whole attitude towards life.

When the intelligences and imaginations of men and women are free from fetters and fears, then they enter the Kingdom.

When they go on discovering, admiring, and playing the noble game of life, they are in the Kingdom.

When they can feast in wonder and praise, they are in the Kingdom. When they have vitality and joy, they are in the Kingdom. When they know that the only true joy is to live in the present moment and not worry about tomorrow, they are in the Kingdom.

When they have developed all their human faculties and become totally human, they are in the Kingdom.

When men and women become fully alive to the presence of God within them and to their own presence in God, then they become divine, and dwellers of the Kingdom.

To the King, our King and God, be glory and honor for ever and ever!

Selected Bibliography

(Of works cited in the text)

Diehl, Charles - *Manuel d'art byzantin,* cited as *History of Byzantine Art* (second edition, 2 volumes, Paris, 1925-26)

Llosky, Vladimir - *In the Image and Likeness of God* (Crestwood, NY, SVS Press, 1974))

Meyendorff, John - *A Study of Gregory Palamas* (London, Faith Press, 1964)

Ousspensky, Leonid - *Theology of the Icon* (Crestwood, NY, SVS Press, 1978)

Ousspensky, Leonid & Llosky, Vladimir - *The Meaning of Icons* (Boston, Boston Book and Art Shop, 1969; *Revised Edition,* Crestwood, NY, SVS Press, 1983)

Payne, Robert - *The Holy Fire* (New York, Harper and Bros., 1957)

Raya, Archbishop Joseph - *The Eyes of the Gospel* (Denville, NJ, Dimension Books, 1978)

Rice, Tamara - *Russian Icons* (Harmondsworth, Thames and Hudson, 1947)

Ware, Father Kallistos - *The Orthodox Way* (Crestwood, NY, SVS Press, 1979)